Helene Brembeck, Karin M. Ekström,
Magnus Mörck (Eds.)

Little Monsters

LITTLE MONSTERS

(De)coupling assemblages of consumption

edited by

Helene Brembeck
Karin M. Ekström
Magnus Mörck

LIT

Gedruckt auf alterungsbeständigem Werkdruckpapier entsprechend
ANSI Z3948 DIN ISO 9706

Cover photo: Magnus Mörck

The authors wish to thank The Bank of Sweden Tercentenary Foundation for funding the project *Commercial Cultures in an Ethnological and Economical Perspective* and the publishing of this book.

Bibliographic information published by the Deutsche Nationalbibliothek
The Deutsche Nationalbibliothek lists this publication in the Deutsche Nationalbibliografie; detailed bibliographic data are available in the Internet at http://dnb.d-nb.de.

ISBN 978-3-8258-0281-3

A catalogue record for this book is available from the British Library

Auslieferung/Verlagskontakt:
Fresnostr. 2 48159 Münster
Tel. +49 (0)251–62 03 20 Fax +49 (0)251–23 19 72
e-Mail: lit@lit-verlag.de http://www.lit-verlag.de

Distributed in the UK by: Global Book Marketing, 99B Wallis Rd, London, E9 5LN
Phone: +44 (0) 20 8533 5800 – Fax: +44 (0) 1600 775 663
http://www.centralbooks.co.uk/acatalog/search.html

Distributed in North America by:

Transaction Publishers
New Brunswick (U.S.A.) and London (U.K.)

Transaction Publishers
Rutgers University
35 Berrue Circle
Piscataway, NJ 08854

Phone: +1 (732) 445 - 2280
Fax: + 1 (732) 445 - 3138
for orders (U. S. only):
toll free (888) 999 - 6778
e-mail:
orders@transactionspub.com

Content

Shopping with Humans and Non-humans. 1
Helene BREMBECK, Karin M. EKSTRÖM and Magnus MÖRCK

I Inspired Monsters

The Power of Design – Allies Fighting Design Exclusion. . . . 15
Lena HANSSON

Modeling Small Scale Utopias. 29
Magnus MÖRCK

II Monster Playgrounds

Setting the Example – Building Privileged Trajectories in Interior Decoration Stores 51
Maria BRODIN

To Consume and Be Consumed 67
Helene BREMBECK

III Precious Monsters

Wedding in a Box – Foldings of Time and Space 89
Eva KNUTS

Creation and Transformation of Value 107
Karin M. EKSTRÖM

IV Monsters Pointing

Fashion and Style in a Commercial and Cultural Borderland . .131
Barbro JOHANSSON

A Tale of a Car Sharing Organization (CSO) Monster. 149
Pernilla JONSSON

Afterword 165
Alison J. CLARKE

References. 167

Biography 181

Shopping with Humans and Non-humans

Helene BREMBECK, Karin M. EKSTRÖM and Magnus MÖRCK

The four-year journey resulting in this book, *Little Monsters* – despite its title not primarily for children – was based on the concept 'commercial culture', as discussed in the book with the same name published by Berg in 2000 (Jackson et. al., 2000). Some of the contributors later lectured or presented papers in Göteborg (Ekström and Brembeck, 2004, 2005). Just as the authors of *Commercial Cultures* went for circuits and flows, leakage, rather than stasis, we move along scenes and settings that are developing. From commercial cultures we borrowed their sustained attempt to move beyond dichotomies like culture and economy or production and consumption. For this, we – as many others – find both reasons of theory and observable changes occurring in the economic field (Firat and Venkatesh, 1995; Löfgren and Willim, 2005).

Here is our version of how to approach matters of consumption presented, profiting from past experience without – hopefully – appearing too fuzzy or falling into the most obvious boxes or traps. Although lacking all pretensions of orthodoxy, this is a post-structuralist endeavor for developing some themes of interest in consumption as we think it can be fruitfully understood. As already subtly suggested, we have been influenced by the writings of many researchers in the cultural studies or material culture tradition, like Alison Clark, Daniel Miller, Frank Mort, Marianne Lien and Orvar Löfgren. But important ideas also filtered down the hill where the Center for Consumer Science (CFK) is geographically situated at its foot. There, on the top, Barbara Czarniawska and colleagues of researchers of organizing have developed tools for studying complex processes of translation (Czarniawska and Sevón, 1996). The *Actor Network Theory* of Bruno Latour has been an important reference point to us (Latour, 1999). This book is a serious attempt to apply a simple ANT approach to consumption. It is an original approach, since research in this field has seen very few applications of this line of work, apart from Cochoy 2004 and 2005. Little Monsters are what consumption is about – processes of translation, fragile entities being created by passing connections that constitute their bodies and limbs.

Finding out about paradoxes

Consumption was always about change – like commodities on a market are exchanged, change hands and get used up. Modernist theorizing showed the workings of this passage from one stage to another, accompanied by conceptual switches like 'from mass-produced goods to singularized or personalized object' or 'from exchange value to use value', all based on the idea that markets are as cold as people consuming are warm from that human stuff, culture. Daniel Miller points to the theorizing in this field moving from a strong polarization to complex but integrated forms where culture often turns out to be the product of commerce (Jackson et. al., 2000). His book *A Theory of Shopping* (1998), a modern classic, offers a great example of this hybridization brought about by a complete reversal of the traditional binary understanding of consumption. The cultural component, the gift, appeared in its most calculating aspect, while the market behavior of provisioning served as the main proof of love and generosity among the London housewives studied. This important book, among others, serves to underline the obvious need for studies that open themselves to complication.

In marketing departments, at universities as well as at companies, a management perspective has traditionally outweighed a consumer perspective. At business schools as well as at companies, production has been seen as overruling consumption. The consumer behavior odyssey during 1986 (Belk et al., 1991) led to a paradigm shift in the academic world. To study consumption and consumers required ethnographic research. Also, the Consumer Culture Theory (CCT) (Arnould and Thompson, 2005) is an attempt to frame a distinctive body of theoretical knowledge about consumption and marketplace behaviors from a combined market and culture perspective.

Another misconception is markets, which often are seen from a utilitarian view thereby neglecting the intermingled relations, powers and networks. Although markets have boundaries in the perception of an actor, these boundaries are given neither solely by the company, the product nor the individual consumer, but should be looked upon as interrelated components making up the agency (Håkansson, Harrison and Waluszewski, 2004).

Moving on from this point we found ANT an attractive companion, since this heterogeneous body of work really proves to be open to all kinds of combinations. Entities that in conventional approaches are taken for granted, such as consumers, goods and companies are here brought into the middle of the spotlight. Consumers are no more to be understood as naked choosing subjects; instead they are made up of assemblies together with other people, goods and companies. Here unstable assemblages are formed, our little monsters. Agency is a question of capabilities that arise within these new combinations, out of a network, not stably residing inside a given actor. Latour has voiced second thought on his choice of key concepts in naming Actor Network Theory. The point should be to see how agency is something that comes out of assembling an actor – rather than the other way around. Also the concept of network is misleading since it seems to imply things like stable electric cables or the clear lines of a highway connecting different points in space. The network should instead be conceptualized as changing and in need of constant attention (Latour, 1999; Czarniawska, 2004).

ANT was developed through the study of laboratories and technological projects, places far from the concerns of everyday consumption, raising some doubts about its applicability to ordinary citizens' lives (Law, 1991). Of necessity it could not provide all the tools for developing consumer research. Our brand of ANT deployed here is somewhat changed by putting more emphasis on culture and discourse than usual. On this point Bruno Latour is somewhat ascetic to our minds – but a more detailed account of our reasoning follows at the end of this introduction.

The tales of consumption

We don't suggest that our approach is all new, since we brought along parts of the tradition of consumer culture studies in ethnology and marketing to work in tandem with ANT. Our work is about developing consumer culture studies by bringing in ANT – not the other way around. The objects of our study, our monsters, do not arise spontaneously from the material collected. There are no endings or beginnings in the networks so the object of study must be created by framing. Our motivation when selecting research questions comes from many different sources of inspiration, but most of it seems to fit well with the tradition. Activities like ritual, collecting, fashion, consumer reforms and collective consumption are all old concerns of consumer researchers. The examples studied provide a great repertoire of narratives: like the Grimm brothers or H. C. Andersen, we are eager to tell the tales of consumption! Good stories are filled with eye-opening stuff, surprises, the twists of the unexpected right out of the Twilight zone. We meet materialistic children or parents creating an intimate moment within the premises of a giant like McDonald's (Helene Brembeck); car poolers trying to get out of the grip of individual transportation (Pernilla Jonsson); young couples imagining a home in that odd reversal of private space, the furniture store (Maria Brodin) or people passing on their cherished collection of radiantly sparkling glass at an auction (Karin M. Ekström); grown men practicing a hobby so close to childhood that it causes unease (Magnus Mörck); children doing age at the intersection of childhood and youth, using their bodies, money, fashion and brands (Barbro Johansson); weddings kept alive as miniature memorabilia in boxes of satin and lace (Eva Knuts) and, finally but first in this book, a designer's dream, in a world full of difference, a plea for commodities that would literally exclude no one (Lena Hansson). These examples line up as our monsters, ready to act out the drama.

Good tales are about looking differently at large companies often ascribed great permanency and power beyond reach of the consumers. Good stories are about questioning consumers too, their decisions, no-decisions and freedom of choice. What if consumers are seen as made up of fleeting assemblies of both matter and spirit? What if agency comes out of alliances between bodies and technology, rather than the other way around? Consumption has sometimes been exposed to good intentions and clever reform. What if we look closer, what can we learn from the paradoxical behavior of the reformers themselves? Are they really developing the networks that best serve their aims as stated in discourse?

The disposition of the chapters makes up four themes. *Inspired Monsters* tell of consumer utopias, good but hard to reach – among designers and also, quite differently among hobbyists, perhaps a case of hopeful monsters that John Law wrote about in A *Sociology of Monsters* (1991), a book that also inspired us. *Monster Playgrounds* revolves around a clearly identified slice of space: a restaurant and a furniture store, respectively. Assembling and ordering attractive objects create value in two cases of *Precious Monsters*, memorabilia for weddings contained for future needs and collectors displaying their loved treasures of art glass. Finally we meet *Monsters Pointing* passionately in a certain direction towards future goals, but not utopian this time. It is shown how children as consumers of fashion adjust their tastes to fit their conceptions and other's expectations, an individual consumer is created – in contrast to the car pool were the consumer is made up of many bodies, that is paradoxically too homogenous to grow as diversified as expected.

Our disciplinary assemblage

The academic disciplines represented in this volume, marketing and ethnology, have traditionally hinged on each side of the market-culture fence, confirming the division between culture and economy. Marketing traditionally studies consumption in terms of markets and consumers to be conquered and managed. A fuller understanding of consumers as actors with dreams and aspirations is thereby historically neglected. The consumer is seen as passive rather than active making his/her own choices. Ethnology traditionally side with the consumers to the extent of rarely acknowledging the creative part played by producers and retailers.

Consumption and different forms of market behavior have historically been consistently addressed in terms of resistance – implying that no give and take between producers and consumers is possible. From this critical cultural perspective there is a definite split between perceiving the everyday life of ordinary people as good and the markets as bad, unless, as often in cultural studies, the focus has been on the individual playing with consumption, creating identities by the use of commodities. These two modernist stories are basically the same, only assigning different value to what is thought to happen. Marketers and ethnologists co-operating have seemed to resemble a successful formula for moving beyond this stuffy binarism. It has also been practiced before us, by representatives of the two disciplines around Lund University (Löfgren and Willim, 2005). Ethnology and marketing seem to make a good couple – they are different, but not too far apart. In the USA, there are anthropologists that happen to work in marketing departments, but surprisingly not the other way around. Work by Eric Arnould, Janeen Costa, John Sherry and Craig Thompson has been an important inspiration for us at CFK. During this four-year project, one of the most widely read and traveled of these border crossers, Russell Belk stayed with us as a guest professor and also became honorary member of CFK. At Association of Consumer Research Conferences in Dublin, Toronto, Portland, Göteborg and Monterrey we were able to collect inspiration from experienced researchers doing cultural studies right in the middle of schools of commerce, as we are doing ourselves. We were especially enthused by the interpretive gatherings preceding ACR called Heretical consumer research, founded by Alladi Venkatesh and Fuat Firat, who also established the journal *Consumption, Markets and Culture*, which inspires us greatly. The special brand of US consumer cultural studies called Consumer Culture Theory (Arnould and Thompson, 2005) has also been important for the development of this field of study.

New perspectives develop partly by the withering away and erosion of old comforting truths. For our predecessors, a lot of energy has gone into proving that a cold environment could house living people who wrestled anonymous and mass-produced goods out of the hands of bad, bad markets to invent their own cultural meanings. Our story is literally less human, since it appears less necessary to rehearse this divide between markets and humans as consumers. With Bruno Latour it has become more interesting to look at humans and non-humans interacting, making up new entities with fleeting permanency, networking in a continuous flow.

In this book we have tried to explore consumption as a number of connected networks involving goods and transactions of value. Networks with different basis, linking actants across traditional divides like the state, the market and everyday life, networks or assemblages that can be more or less firmly or loosely coupled and that are organized with different objectives in mind: they might be about making everyday life bearable, getting dinner on the table everyday for the family: for companies they might be about making people buy your products: for the activist they might be about enrolling others to sustainable ways of producing and consuming. These networks or assemblages might be about me and my stuff or be global and involve millions of actants.

The entities, actants, human as well as non-human, have no essential characteristics, but become or are given agency in relation to other actants. Humans, goods or ideas e.g., traveling around the world are changed, translated or performed, differently, in every new meeting with others. What connects the actants and what is also used by the actants in order to enroll others to their network or assemblage are primarily texts, technical artifacts, humans and money that are used as intermediaries. Important in order to become a powerful macro actor is the number of so-called black boxes which the actor is able to enroll. Black boxes contain non-questionable certainties, things that are taken for granted, about for example children and consumption. Actors that are able to pile up many black boxes, increase their power and their possibilities of becoming dominant actors.

Everything starts in the middle

Networks differ in being firm or loose. Businesses can be understood as firmly coupled networks, in various ways trying to connect to humans, things and technologies, or as settings where central actors are trying to organize the network in such a way that goods can be produced and consumers are able to connect themselves. Everyday life also contains many firmly coupled networks. The daily grocery shopping, the division of household labor in the family might be much ritualized, the same way as goods themselves are main actors in many lifecycles or seasonal rituals, like weddings. Other networks or assemblages are loosely coupled, which is often the case for networks involving or connecting consumers and producers. Such networks might be very fragile and elusive. In the store there are a huge amount of entities that might be coupled in more or less unpredictable ways, the customers of course and the goods for sale, but also the state by means of information on the packages, moreover the shopping trolleys, the display cases guiding the customers through the shop, the bar code that only the digital eye of the cash register can interpret. In the store, such as the interior decoration store mentioned in this book, moreover a number of networks are coupled, families looking at furniture to bring home, goods circulating, chains of distribution, heaps of wood, cloth, plastic and aluminum from faraway places, ecological and fair-trade labeling, Swedish couples in their living room sofas and the workers of third-world cotton and tree plantations, getting money for picking cotton or cutting trees for our designer chairs and tables, that they might use to buy stuff on the local market, maybe even worn out children's clothes from some charitable organization in Sweden. This way all things mesh together. Everything starts in the middle; there is no obvious beginning or cause. By following chains of people and things and by studying the way alliances are made, we believe it is possible to gain a fuller understanding of the conditions of consumption and what living in a consumer culture involves.

By being located geographically in the same space and interacting regularly at meetings as well as coffee breaks, both thoughts and perspiration have created a radiating atmosphere making interdisciplinary exchange possible. The examples in this book could equally well be studied as markets and as cultures, and would certainly have been so, unless this interdisciplinary effort had not been realized. The prime difference between the two is where you put your frame. If you are interested in networks of people and things enabling transactions, markets are a preferred model. If you are interested in the performance of meanings, probably by those same actors, your choice would be culture. Different relations are inevitably framed, and the same way the world turns into markets for marketers, society for the sociologist or nature for the biologist, it turns into culture for the ethnologist. We would however like to keep the option open.

But don't forget

ANT developed from the idea of giving voice to non-humans, often very complicated technological artifacts and its preferred scenery was the laboratory and later companies and all kinds of organizing efforts. Consumption is of course also an activity that takes a lot of co-ordination from producers, retailers and their customers, but culture and meaning seems somehow to be underestimated, as far as we are concerned, and here we agree with sociologist Mike Michael's comments on Latour (2000).

Politics is a more established part of ANT discovering new parliaments in areas like technology or fashion (Latour and Weibel, 2005). Consumer society in itself has been instrumental in bringing about a scene where ideologies and social groups have lost their coherence. It is often noted that politics has become consumption in a negative sense that seems to exclude any prolonged engagements with the profound problems created by global consumerism. These networks are difficult to grasp, even the simplest commodity is assembled of components from many different countries, thereby eroding the possibilities of old-fashioned politics. But with ANT it seems possible to trace politics arising in new areas, like Cochoy in his studies of consumers, producers, the law and NGOs circling around legal packages and shopping carts in the supermarket (Cochoy, 2004, 2005). Ideas and movements have appeared because of globalization and make up an important part of the present form of consumerism. It is also necessary to go beyond the simple conception of consumer society as simply hedonistic pleasure. Shopping is not just pleasure and in everyday life several ambivalent responses to the many negative sides of consumer society appear. The further commoditization of human needs also creates a scene for criticism and reflexivity. It is important to charter these developments, even if weak and disparate. In ANT terms politics is not created in some distant parliamentary sphere, but as a part of the assemblages that make up large-scale consumption, like the failed public transport system Latour studied in *Aramis or the Love of Technology* (1993). Here is our attempt at consumer culture studies with ethics and politics as well as heart and delight.

Box of concepts

Following is a brief list of the ANT inspired concepts or tools most frequently used in this book. We do not aim at a thorough analysis of the many ways they have been defined and discussed. Our ambition is simply to give the reader an idea of how we have come to understand and practice them throughout the project and use them in this book.

Actant: The smallest parts of a network. Entities that can be both human and non-human.

Actor: As pointed out by Czarniawska and Hernes (2005) not everybody acting become independent actors with an own voice, but many are part of networks acting like actors. Although we use actant and actor more or less in parallel, we are primarily concerned with actors of various kinds performing and performed by relations in actor-networks. All of our monsters are, become or aspire to become actors.

Actor-network: Assemblages of actors, that can be large or small, loosely or firmly coupled, elusive or stable, from small gadgets and toys (Johansson and Brembeck) and the wedding keepsake boxes in Eva Knut's chapter that are not supposed to be opened too often, the relatively larger carpool (Jonsson) and auction (Ekström), and finally the almost world-wide, elusive and instable networks of Universal Design (Hansson) or paper craft hobbyists (Mörck).

Agency: An actor is not an agent in itself and has no given identity outside of the actor-network in which its agency or non-agency is performed. All entities achieve their form as a consequence of the relations in which they are located; they are performed in, by, and through those relations. The agency of 'becoming-teenager Fredrik' in Barbro Johansson's chapter is performed in an assemblage of designer clothes and hairstyles, and the 'store-living room' in Maria Brodin's chapter is performed by repeated orderings of seemingly inconsistent actants in the interior decoration store.

Co(a)gent: We have used this concept proposed by Mike Michael (2000) to remind us of the fact that the actors of our study – our monsters – and their agencies are always distributed in time and space, they are coagents with coagency, at the same time as they are concentrated actors, or following Michael, cogents with cogency comprising the co(a)gent, just like the birthday child in Helene Brembeck's chapter can be regarded as a concentrated or even singular agent/agency at the same time as she/he is distributed in time and space, or the cogency of the 'girl-thongs' in Barbro Johansson's chapter is also a distributed assemblage of bodies, ages and gazes.

Trajectory: The drift, movement, path or ordering of any entity or actor. An example from Brodin's chapter is the building of paths – orderings – in the interior decoration store in the performance of the store-living room or the diverse and competing orderings of the birthday party by company, staff and children in Brembeck's chapter.

Translation: Movement or spread in time and space occurs by displacement, drift, invention, mediation, which is the creation of a new link that did not exist before, and modifies in part the two agents. The old paper craft dolls and houses in Magnus Mörck's chapter are translated into PDF files on homepages and web-rings on the internet, and once again translated from two dimensional models into three dimensional objects in the hands of eager hobbyists, downloading them from the internet.

Inscription/prescription: As shown in Lena Hansson's chapter on Universal Design, designers make inscriptions of how artifacts should work and look like with an imagined user and context in mind, inscriptions that are materialized as prescriptions, i.e. what the object allows, or forbids actors and what they anticipate. This also gives the objects a certain kind of morality, both negative (what they proscribe), and positive (what they permit) (Akrich, 1992; Latour, 1992).

Affordance: The surface or structure making up an actor's environment and specifying a range of possible actions for that actor. We have been inspired by Michael's application highlighting that such possible actions also reflect the capacities and limits of the acting body (Michael 2000). The tubes in the party room at McDonald's in Brembeck's chapter affords the children to climb, crawl, slide, and run upwards, and downwards in ways not possible for the larger and stiffer bodies of adults.

Enrollment: The connecting of new actants/actors to a network by way of encounters (trials of force). This is the way the Universal Design movement (Hansson) and the paper craft web-rings (Mörck) grow, as well as the carpool in Pernilla Jonsson's chapter trying to enroll consumers with the help of green ideology, easily accessible cars and inexpensive driving. As pointed out by Czarniawska and Hernes (2005) actors also acquire a distinct and relatively stable character due to successful enrollment: the formation and stabilization of networks of actants, who can then present themselves as actors. The wedding in Eva Knut's chapter has been stabilized by putting memorabilia in a keepsake box and locking it up.

Framing: The drawing of a clear and precise boundary between the relations which are taken into account on the one hand, and the multitude of relations which will be ignored on the other (Callon, 1997). The auction in Karin M. Ekström's chapter has no clear boundary, but has to be framed by the author before analyzing it, just like the birthday party (Brembeck), the Universal Design movement (Hansson) or the hobbyists interacting on the internet (Mörck).

Blackbox: contains that which no longer needs to be considered, those things whose contents have become a matter of indifference (Callon and Latour, 1981), such as the privately owned car (Jonsson) and the gender and generational orderings (Brembeck, Johansson) are. A blackbox, therefore, is any setting that no matter how complex it is or how contested its history has been, is now so stable and certain that it can be treated as a fact where only the input and output counts.

Monster: Our playful name for the commercial culture assemblages we are framing, like the girl-thongs, the store-living room, the miniaturized and boxed weddings, the art glass auction and the green car sharing organization of Majorna, highlighting their hybrid and mixed character bridging culture-economy, everyday culture-commerce and production-consumption divides.

I

Inspired Monsters

The Power of Design – Allies Fighting Design Exclusion

Lena HANSSON

The intent of Universal design is to simplify life for everyone by making products, communications, and the built environment more usable by as many people as possible at little or no extra cost. Universal design benefits people of all ages and abilities. (Center for Universal design)

This statement is found on the Center for Universal design's website (CUD[1] 2007–01–16). It embraces the core value of the design concept 'Universal design'. Emphasizing usability and accessibility for all people, it connotes an ideological view of design and an urge to serve humans and society as a whole. The concept emerged during the 1980's and through the work of advocates such as designers and producers, as well as among representatives from disability rights organizations and politicians, the concept is nowadays globally recognized (Ostroff, 2001).

Statements about Universal design, like the one above, imply that an ideal world in which everyone is included by design is possible to achieve. As this is not the case today, people experience design exclusion (Keates and Clarkson, 2004) when they cannot access or readily use an artifact whether it is a product, service or environment. Who has for instance not felt lost in a new place, have had problems in attempting to handle a new technical device or restrained by a heavy door or something else that makes access difficult? For some it is more troublesome than for others. This makes design exclusion something relative. When consumers are excluded by design they usually get frustrated with themselves rather than blame the object or its design. This self-blame is common even though it could be argued that the design should make sure a user can grasp what to do with an object and be able to use it properly (e.g., Monö, 1997; Norman, 1998). Design exclusion is by advocates assumed to be an unwanted effect of design and something that can be eliminated by using a Universal design approach.

The purpose of this chapter is to follow Universal design as an idea in order to unfold its paths and see how it allies with various actors (humans and non-humans) (e.g., Latour, 1998) like advocates, ideas, documents, design processes, politics, ethics, et cetera, creating an actor network, a monster

1 CUD – The Center for Universal design, www.design.ncsu.edu/cud/about_ud/about_ud.htm

with good intentions. The chapter will depart from the perspective of designers since they are among the strongest advocates of Universal design (Hansson, 2006). The material embraces interviews with designers and other design experts of Universal design in addition to documents collected on the Internet, as well as literature and handbooks. It consists of material collected for my thesis about Universal design from a consumer research perspective (Hansson, 2006).

The utopian challenge

Ronald Mace, an American architect, was the first to use the term Universal design in 1985 (Ostroff, 2001) and formulated the idea like this:

> Universal design is the design of products and environments to be usable by all people, to the greatest extent possible, without the need for adaptation or specialized design. (Ostroff, 2001)

This specific definition is stated in many documents relating to Universal design (e.g., Paulsson, 2000; Aslaksen, et al. 1997), both within different design areas and various organizations. It is either used in its identical form or with some minor changes made in the formulation. It seems to be the most unifying reference for designers promoting Universal design.

An idea can be materialized in many ways, both in objects and as actions, but first it must be known, and it comes to exist in the form of words or pictures (Czarniawska and Joerges, 1996). Universal design comes to exist in the materialized world through the translation of the mental image of the idea into words. These words stated in documents and other texts become what Latour (1999) calls 'circulating references', i.e. materialized objects of the idea. They work as intermediaries between the idea and the designers. In connection with human actors, these circulating references receive non-human agency and work in favor of a Universal design approach.

Nevertheless, the idea of Universal design is in its formulation open for negotiations: 'the design of products and environments to be usable by all people, to the greatest extent possible, without the need for adaptation or specialized design'. What does usable mean? Who are 'all' people? What is 'the greatest extent possible'? The interviewed designers explain that for some people even the very term 'universal' is provocative as it implies the possibility to create designed artifacts that everyone can use. If people are provoked it is because they take the idea literally and they may then question the possibility to achieve

Universal design in practice. The idea may also be rejected as a non-desirable approach as it also seems to work against the use of design as a market differentiator. The industry segments their markets and uses design to offer different alternatives for consumers to choose among. Design is an important competitive tool for the industry (Kotler and Rath, 1984) as well as a means of satisfying consumer needs for individualization and differentiation (e.g., Gabriel and Lang, 1995). If taken literally, the idea is therefore easy to reject. Another reason for dismissing the idea is if it is associated with design for special users, as assistive aid or design for disabled (e.g., Welsh, 1995; Leibrock and Terry, 1999).

The interviewed designers are aware of these reasons for dismissal and argue that Universal design should not be taken literally as a "one size fits all" standard. The intention is neither to target consumers with specific disabilities. Instead, Universal design should be something to strive for with the ambition of including as many as possible. However, the utopian ambition is considered in a realistic light – designers cannot embrace everyone in every situation or at any time. What is important is rather to be aware of whom you as a designer exclude with a design. Otherwise, design exclusion cannot be counteracted and people are discriminated.

From a designer perspective this means that using a Universal design approach can be viewed as taking one step towards a better world. This is communicated through the designed artifacts as these are assumed to implicitly communicate the moral of its creator and the social ideology behind it (Akrich, 1992). It is therefore not uncommon among the interviewed designers to see it as their mission to spread the idea of Universal design and take on an educational role to get the message out:

> The problem with Universal design is that people are not always aware of the significance and the need for it. It also requires knowledge and a conscious attitude and design methodology. But if the client is not aware of this, the educational work is also important. (Mona)

Obviously when talking about Universal design, advocates need to explain not only what it is about but also what it is not about. The misinterpretation of the idea is partly a discursive problem, since what is said in relation to Universal design has impact on how it is perceived. A consequence of this is that it becomes harder for those already allied to convince other potential actors to become an ally. Equally important is that at the same time as the idea may intimidate and provoke some, it is inviting for others as it opens up the possibility of making a difference.

The doing of design – making inscriptions stable

Although designers may believe in the idea of Universal design they also need to translate it in their practice. In their work, designers make inscriptions of how artifacts should work and look like by their decisions about the form et cetera and these inscriptions are materialized in the artifacts as prescriptions, function and what it allows or forbids the actor to do (Akrich, 1992; Latour, 1992).

In the practice of design, the idea of Universal design is translated when designers try to visualize it in the design process. The transformation of the formulated idea (in words) into a designed object happens through a chain of translations. For instance, the Universal design idea has been translated into seven guiding principles for the design practice. These are (1) Equitable use, (2) Flexibility in use, (3) Simple and intuitive use, (4) Perceptible information, (5) Tolerance for error, (6) Low physical effort, and (7) Size and space for approach and use (Story, Mueller and Mace, 1998).

Each principle of Universal design fulfills different requirements that a designed artifact should 'live up to'. Besides guiding a design process, these principles can also be used as a diagnostic tool for evaluation. The second principle 'flexible in use' for example is described as "design that accommodates a wide range of individual preferences and abilities" (Story et al., 1998). A pair of scissors should then be able to accommodate both right-handed and left-handed, those with smaller hands as well as bigger hands, and with crocked hands etc. Preferably they should also be able to be used safely and without too much physical effort which corresponds to both the fifth and sixth principle.

When reviewing the principles they clearly emphasize design aspects like function, usability and accessibility which in some respect are commonly considered in many design processes. The difference is that the Universal design principles include an ambition to cover a great range of human abilities in order to create designed artifacts that are functional, usable and accessible for more people. Even so, as the second principle shows, they are rather generally formulated and do not specify exactly which preferences and abilities that should be considered. On the other hand, their formulation creates possibilities of applying them to many different kinds of artifacts. A public place like a town square for instance, needs to be designed with many different abilities in mind since it is assumed to be used by all citizens. It is somewhat different for a consumer product like a kitchen knife as it is possible to satisfy different consumer needs by making a range of kitchen knives. These different conditions for a design might result in different levels of 'universal' qualities.

If used in the design process, the principles of Universal design are translated into inscriptions by designers and thus work as actors to make designed objects more 'universal'. In this way they can be considered the 'right way' to do things in order to reach a more 'inclusive' design. But the principles are presented as recommendations and if and how they are considered are still up to the designers. Not all of the interviewed designers use the principles explicitly but they are all strong advocates of the embedded aspects, i.e. function, usability, and accessibility. However, in a design process these design aspects, embraced in the principles, are negotiated over other design aspects like aesthetics et cetera (Story et al., 1998). Nevertheless, the ideological standpoint of Universal design with its 'inclusive' thought ought to influence the aesthetics of a 'universal' artifact.

For the interviewed designers the aesthetics of Universal design should ideally elucidate the function, the design should give clues of how to handle an artifact in order to make it usable and accessible. They see no contradiction between creating a 'universal' artifact and an aesthetically pleasant artifact at the same time. It may be a design challenge but something designers should be able to face.

> I don't think anything is good if it isn't both beautiful and functional. I have seen very few products that fulfill both these requirements but I think it's more an inability because a designer should be able to handle both parts. (Berit)

It is also emphasized that a 'universal' artifact should not stigmatize, and should not deviate from the design of similar artifacts, but should support all users in a simple and invisible way (Welsh 1995: iii). This implies that Universal design should not be viewed as something special but should really be integrated into mainstream design. And this makes sense; since it is not until then consumers that today are excluded by design will become truly included.

But a major challenge is how to translate 'all people' into the design process. This I believe is the true utopian ambition and in design practice this becomes obvious. When talking about the practice of Universal design most of the interviewed designers turn out to still invite mostly people with different disabilities to participate in the design process. Some of them argue that working with these groups also provide other user groups with more accessible environments or easily handled products.

> What is good for those with the greatest problem is good for everyone, and it should work for everyone – you don't have to come up with special solutions. A typical reservation is to create a special website for those who can't see, without pictures and without integrating it, which is a typical example for me. The thought isn't to have a kitchen entrance for one who can't walk but to build a ramp at the main entrance instead. It's the same when it comes to the web, the main entrance should be made for as many as possible to enter, then clearly for those with severe disabilities...I mean 'for all' that is more utopia. (Anna)

This statement illustrates the moral and ethical view of people that the interviewed designers share. The idea of Universal design definitely opens up and questions the 'black box' of how to conceptualize people.

The working of design exclusion

In the interaction with artifacts, people are trained to behave in a certain way. We have learnt a behavior 'program', a symbolic language, to understand artifacts and how to do things. This embodied skill is used each time we interact with an artifact. We then follow a pre-described program but the first time we experience a new artifact, a new program must be learnt or we may try an old one that seems suitable for a similar artifact. If the program does not work we may try to adapt, but it still might not work as expected. Or we may not even be able to use the artifact in question at all. Something has then gone wrong in the translation chain.

For instance, most people know how to open a door, so whenever you reach a door you know by earlier experience that this is a door and how to open it. However, in times of increased need of security you find many doors looked and alarmed. You therefore need to press a button (marked with the symbol of a key) in order to open the door. To reduce the possibility of misbehavior the door lock is covered with a plastic shelter which prevents the alarm from starting. Several clues are given here to make it possible to open the door and they are a part of the program 'to open a door' and every sign, material, symbolic, or verbalized is part of the translation chain. These clues rely on a shared symbolic language among actors, for instance designers, manufacturers, as well as users/consumers in order for it to work.

Furthermore, even if you might understand how to unlock the door this does not necessarily mean you are able to enter it. It might either require too much effort to open or be too narrow you to pass through. The solution is a door that is opened automatically so that nobody has to use any effort to enter, which undermines discrimination not only for people in wheel chairs, people with rheumatism and/or children but also for people who have their hands occupied with a stroller or bags. In this way the prescriptions are made less restrictive by delegating parts of the program to a non-human actant, the door opener (Latour, 1992) and the result is a more user-friendly device for more people. But considering the range of possible prescriptions and subscriptions to make, the experience of an object is hard to predict. The designed artifact is in the state of 'becoming' (see also Johansson in this volume), before it has been given its final form, as well as later on in every meeting with a consumer.

User misbehavior can be defined as an 'anti-program', whether it is due to lack of competence or poor design. Consumers might try to use the artifact in a non-prescribed way or they may just not understand how to behave/use it. If this is the case, there exists a gap between the prescriptions and the subscriptions (how consumers react to what is prescribed). It is when a user neither understands how to use an artifact nor is able to use it, that he or she becomes excluded by design. As a consumer you might feel stigmatized or handicapped when you do not live up to the requirements set by the design, even if it happens to be poor design, that is less inclusive. The video recorder is an excellent example of a particular technical device that is often mentioned by consumers (e.g., Keates and Clarkson, 2004) as problematic for them. If you do not know how to handle your video recorder you become 'handicapped'. This indicates that anyone irrespective of dis/ability or competence and experience design exclusion from time to time and in different situations for various reasons (Hansson, 2006).

In a perfect world each and every individual's needs and wants would be considered and satisfied by the design of artifacts whether it is built environments, products, services et cetera. Since this is not the case, consumers are excluded by design. Design exclusion which can be either physical or mental may in turn lead to cultural and social exclusion as well since the possibility of excluded consumers living the life that they want diminishes. Especially since consumers view designed artifacts as a means of creating a meaningful life as well as an individual lifestyle (Lury, 1997).

Enable consumers

The view of consumers, i.e. users, is of great importance in the design process and advocates of Universal design object to the traditional segregation and stereotyping of people who do not fit 'the norm', such as children, elderly, and disabled. What seems important for the designers though is to try and go beyond disability, not to distinguish between disabled and 'abled' people. Instead, everyone should be considered so that everyone has the same possibilities.

We are individuals, we are of different height, we have different hearing abilities, and we also hear differently in different situations, and we see differently in different situations. In the morning when it's dark in the bedroom it can be hard to see the time if it isn't well-lit, or if the contrasts are not good et cetera. In other situations we can easily see the time. It's the same for those who are visually impaired, in certain situations their sight is great and in other cases they get really dazzled, which is more disturbing than anything else for one person but not for another. (Harald)

The extent of consumers' problems with designed artifacts varies and could be discussed in terms of dis/ability. According to Moser and Law (1999) it is in the assemblage of bodies and designed artifacts the character of dis/ability is affected or even constructed. They explain that if you have the corporeal ability to turn your television on and off, choose a channel to watch, decide how loud the sound should be, you feel able. But this is possible also with a material specificity as a joystick that makes it possible to control the functions of the television even without all corporeal abilities. Being able makes it possible for people to live independent lives, but feeling able is just as important, as it influences our self-image. Therefore, it is usually better to be what Moser and Law refer to as 'a standardized bodily package', one that is normatively approved, because such bodies can perform naturally and smoothly in the network of materialized specificities. In this way the bodies are made invisible.

The body becomes on the other hand very visible in the network if it is non-standardized as the assemblages with non-human actants are not working according to a prescribed program. For instance, as Moser and Law exemplifies: stairs don't mix with wheelchairs, they mix better with legs. Although it requires many assemblages with the right material, human and non-human, it is possible to become able even with a non-standardized body but this is often made impossible because of design exclusion. Design can in this way both empower or disempower people. It is interesting to note that a lot of material objects are required to become free from one's bodily restraints. This is why design can make a difference for the everyday life of consumers. How design is viewed thus becomes important.

Enrolling the market monster

Universal design can be viewed as a visionary declaration but it can also be seen as a utopian challenge and impossible to achieve. This is one reason for the resistance among actors outside the Universal Design network. The allied designers need to 'fight' against people who are not convinced about the excellence of the idea. One way of doing this is to try and enroll the market. According to Mace (cited by Reagan, 1998) Universal design is design for the built environment and consumer products for a very broad definition of a user that encourages attractive, marketable products that are more usable for everyone. Universal design should in this way be viewed as an issue driven by the consumer market and a way of broadening mainstream. It should therefore not be viewed as a special kind of design but could be integrated in any design process.

Another commonly used market argument when arguing for Universal design is the demographic change of aging populations in many European countries as well as in USA and Japan. By 2010, for instance, one in five Europeans will be aged 62 and over (Eurostat: 101) and every second European will be over 50 years old in 2020 (Coleman, 1999). The future masses of aging bodies ought to become a strong actor in the network, driving the demand for more 'universal' artifacts. With aging come inevitable changes in abilities. The overwhelming majority of people with disabilities are older people with minor impairments, problems with hearing or with walking far without aid et cetera, which hinder everyday activities (Green and Jordan, 1999). Their power as consumers will certainly put pressure on the commercial market to change the attitude of the non-standardized body and the design of artifacts.

Until this has been realized actors other than designers and their market practice create problems that must be dealt with. Marketers often work as 'silent designers' as their decisions about market research and target markets have impact on the design process (Gorb and Dumas, 1987). The idea of Universal design might be found as somewhat provocative and perceived as an impossible ambition for them as they are working with well-established principles of segmentation. To reach as many 'customers' as possible within a specific target group with designed offerings they choose certain consumers. The information collected about potential customers, or more commonly about existing customers, is transformed into a 'conceptualized consumer', a typical consumer within the target group. This conceptualization is usually based on too limited generalizations of people (e.g., Moschis, Lee and Mathur, 1997). Furthermore, it is common to define consumers according to their lifestyles, i.e. their interests, attitudes, and opinions (e.g., Holt, 1997). The materialized body is in this case not a great concern as lifestyle aspects are viewed as disconnected from it, but to the extent that it is considered, it is a normatively standardized body that is defined. Within the marketing practice consumers are thus excluded on the grounds of deviating from the normative standardized bodies, first in marketing and then in the following design process.

Therefore, the market practice makes it hard for the Universal design network to connect to this network but is still considered an important actor to ally with because of its close monitoring of consumer desires. Obviously, consumers do not consist of materialized bodies entirely. Consumers are co(a)gents or hybrids of technology, nature, society, culture and bodies. It is as such entities that they act in everyday life together with designed artifacts (Michael, 2000). Designed artifacts not only make consumers' everyday comfortable and bearable, they make it pleasant as well. They also provide consumers with the possibility of communicating important symbolic values about themselves as individuals (e.g., Gabriel and Lang, 1995). Designed artifacts must then function well, but also with style as Schroeder puts it (2002). However, according to the designers there is no contradiction between offering commercial designed artifacts that are usable and accessible to many consumers and on the other hand making them attractive both for their aesthetic and symbolic value.

Connecting to broader networks

The ideology behind Universal design becomes explicit among the interviewed designers when they talk about the idea. They use ethical and morale arguments in their attempt to get members to enroll in the Universal design network. They are referring both to human rights and the new anti-discrimination clause of the EU (e.g., Hansson, 2006). With the aim of achieving equality of opportunity and social inclusion for everyone, the anti-discrimination clause states that actions should be taken against discrimination based on sex, racial or ethical origin, religion or belief, disability, age or sexual orientation and towards physical accessibility (Preiser and Ostroff, 2001; EU Treaty of Amsterdam [2]).

The idea of Universal design is congruent with the human rights and other non-discrimination policies as these also aspire to a more equal world. As declarations they are more powerful than Universal design on a more general level as they are supported by governmental actors but are, like the design concept, far from reaching their goal. Societies are yet not equal and people are discriminated in different ways around the world. Even so, these policies become 'circulating references' within the network of Universal design and are as such useful for actors who attempt to achieve a more equal world by performing different activities. These have for instance resulted in other 'circulating references' which are linked more directly to Universal like the Swedish governmental statements 'Accessibility for all by 2010' and 'An information society for all' [3]. Such statements are used by advocates in order to give them power to enroll new actors into the network. It is one example of how to create a 'program' that works in favor of Universal design.

The idea of Universal design can also be connected to other known design movements with the pursuit of making changes in society with the help of design. Design reflects but also influences societal and cultural values as well as commercial and political interests of its time (Sparke, 1987; Thackara, 1988; Woodham, 1997). The modernists in the latter 19th century believed in creating a democratic ideal society "whereby the majority would be able to enjoy an improved quality of life in a hygienic, healthy, and modern environment" (Woodham, 1997: p34). The modernistic project can in its earliest phase be seen as a social utopian commitment just like the idea of Universal design. The 'modern aesthetics' was characterized by geometric forms, undecorated surfaces, and an attempt to unite function and form (Sparke, 2004). The famous German design school Bauhaus stands as a role model for the modern style and still has an impact on designers in these days even if it is challenged by many other views of design.

Furthermore, the Universal design 'movement' partly resembles the 'social responsible design' movement which started out in the 1960's when the pur-

2 www.itcilo.it/english/actrav/telearn/global/ilo/blokit/eutrety.htm, 2006 – 01 – 27.

3 The Swedish Government Bills: 1999/2000:79: From patient to citizen – a national action plan for the handicap politics requires general accessibility pervading society by 2010. Universal design or the Swedish term Design for All is included as a means of reaching this goal: Government Bill 1999/2000: 86: An information society for all, states that "... everyone must be able to take part in the information society... for people with disabilities it requires that the IT systems are accessible and usable".

pose of design as a differentiator or market-led design (e.g., Whiteley, 1993) was questioned. It was during this time the views of designers like Papanek (1984) became very influential, emphasizing a true user focus and the need to consider minorities including people with disabilities. Such democratic idealism can also be derived from Scandinavia. In Sweden, the design fields of assistive aid emerged in close connection to the field of ergonomics during the late 1960's (Rosell, 1994). These design fields have been strong actors in the Swedish design community ever since then. As they are closely related to the ideology of Universal design, it is not surprising to find that several of the interviewed designers have professional background within these design fields or sympathize with these views of design.

Still, despite the possibility of making references to other design traditions like the ones presented above, the Universal design movement can only be described as a more loosely coupled network than, for instance, Bauhaus. It has never been manifested in an institutionalized system like the design school with a development of both practice and theory. It is neither as strong as the social responsible design movement even it is linked to this network. Instead it is characterized by a multitude of activities like individual design courses, conferences, speeches on conferences and at other seminars, and projects within and outside universities et cetera. They take place all over the world but are often shared among actors within the network over Internet or through other intermediaries. This brings the actors together in assemblages without any given location which strengthens the network globally. Furthermore, in many cases the information and documentation are available for anyone interested, allowing the network to grow as it makes it easy for actors outside the network to enroll.

The hopeful monster of Universal design

Design can be used as a means of change and the monster of Universal design is certainly in pursuit of doing just that. One can look upon the idea of Universal design respectfully because of its utopian ambition even if it may be an unreachable ideal – a dream – but it inspires and challenges the market monster. Utopias fill important roles by creating possible, imaginable futures (Dobers and Strannegård, 2005). For designers, Universal design may be a way to handle the gap between the real and an ideal world. This is something everyone struggles with and to sustain hope, people use something McCracken calls 'displacement of meaning' as it "allows us to suppose that while things may not presently conform to ideal expectations, there is a time or a place in which they do" (1988: 110). It becomes a way to make a difference.

Although if it is obvious that the monster of Universal design has the possibility to achieve something great not much seems to happen. Even if the monster is growing, so far not enough actors, neither people nor non-human actants, have been enrolled to ensure its survival. The idea of Universal design becomes partly weakened in the materializations of the idea as individual objects only have the capacity to encapsulate parts of the entire scope of the idea and may then not even be defined as 'universal'. Many actors have been negotiating during the transformation of the idea into a design. It results in more or less 'universal' designed artifacts depending on to what extent they counteract design exclusion and for whom. With good examples of 'universal' designed artifacts, these work as spokespersons for the network. But it is not until they bond with humans in assemblages that they become powerful actors. So when consumers interact with 'universal' designed objects these objects will work in silence as actors of Universal design. At the same time they must compete and negotiate with similar designed artifacts in circulation connected to other networks.

Although there is a long way to go before all designed objects work in favor of the Universal design idea, one of the strengths with the idea is that it can be translated into many different contexts and practices because of its freedom of interpretation. The utopian ideal of Universal design is therefore to a great extent preserved in the communication of the idea (verbally and in writing). On the other hand, it makes the network unstable and open for negotiations. The Universal design network continues to transform while new associations are being made and conditions are changing. For instance, what is 'universal' design and what is it not? Actors with different interests will continue to negotiate about this. For those who like the idea as a whole it will remain an inspiration and becomes something to strive for.

According to Jordan (1999) an idea has a greater chance to become successful in practice if it fits in with the Zeitgeist or 'the spirit of the age' which means it must be compatible with norms. Considering that one of the most important changes that have brought Universal design to the fore is the aging population of contemporary Western societies, aging people has the potential as a group to become a strong actor within the network. Their numbers imply that they will not remain quiet but will become an important consumer voice as aging requires supportive design in terms of accessibility and usability to live an independent life and remain 'able'. So if the views of elderly have not yet changed they are bound to do so in the near future. Furthermore, since social and cultural acceptance is very important and consumers get it through consumption, the need for more both usable and socially acceptable designed artifacts are required to meet the future demands of these consumers. If the idea of Universal design in assemblages with advocates et cetera can ally with other actors in stronger networks, like the market monster, it may be able to achieve this. However, to ally with the more powerful monster of the market and its practice, the Universal design monster may be weakened. The network will change and the idea of Universal design might become blurred. This could work against the mission of counteracting design exclusion, but it could also transform the monster into something prospering within the network of mainstream design. The prospect of the monster of Universal design is hard to predict.

Maybe it is easier to create an ideal world of miniatures? Magnus Mörck will in the next chapter take us into the world of miniatures to see how small artefacts work as objectification of human ideas.

Modeling Small Scale Utopias

Magnus MÖRCK

Printable downloads started to appear on the web in the mid-eighties, the first artifacts to be reproduced were Apple computers in the form of a little miniature, flattened box to be printed out, cut, scored and folded. These printables were a part of the brand cult of the Mac computer, celebrating its superior design and the early appearance of programs that turned 2-dimensional drawings into 3-dimensional objects by projecting the six sides of a simplified computer monitor into a flattened shape with white tabs for gluing – a card model. This chapter tracks the movements of the tiniest of monsters: it is an ethnography of this expanding world of miniatures as they have come to appear on the web in the form of printable downloads. They are the products of hobbyism, fan cultures, net trading, museums or marketing strategies.

Apparently an heir of the lithographic print medium of the 19th century, this new combination of printing and miniaturization consists of data files posted on homepages, meaning change, adaptation, loss and new possibilities compared to the older medium. The result is a revival of paper technologies that for a long time have been receding as manufacturers of toys and hobby products turned to plastic as the favored mimetic material. Now paper is coming back with the help of the net (hardly surprising considering the profitable partnership between paper and computers). This makes the chapter an excursion into material culture (Miller, 1997), in at least three senses: in terms of the materiality of paper, in terms of the digital plumbing that makes the files circulate (Hine, 2000), and finally also in terms of scale – miniatures is a matter of shrinking the size of objects (Stewart, 1987). Also dealt with, providing the main concerns, and continuing the themes from the preceding chapter, are questions like, how a network is formed, its growth through enrollment, with a special consideration on the part played by desire and seduction. If the movement of Universal design covets democratic accessibility as utopian ideal, the small-scale world of the present chapter also gestures towards this realm. Ideals appear in two main forms, both which will be discussed at length, the first being fragmented and manifold, made public in the objects and bodies reproduced, the second being more general, the fact that miniaturization itself tends to idealize things. In the sense that miniatures are tricky to make, they also embody virtues of diligence and skill. The bonds between humans and miniatures are not without dangers; at the end the ambivalences of the miniature are discussed.

Japanese paper art for downloading, a donut with chocolate and sugar frosting in clever geometrical simplification. Photographer: Magnus Mörck

This project has dealt with both online developments and how objects and relations moved off the net (Mörck, 2006). Christine Hine's (2000) rules for nethnography were used to outline the places and rituals on the web that distribute printable miniatures. Homepages, web rings and albums have been documented. Online exploration was followed up with an ethnography at home (Lally, 2002) – by visiting card model hobbyists and paper doll designers where they lived, in Germany, Holland, Italy, Sweden, Denmark and the USA. Quotations from these interviews are used below. A regular convention of paper modeling held yearly in Bremerhaven, Germany, was also visited several times.

The miniature is not a topic that has attracted much attention. There exist some writings on the miniature in general, inspired by phenomenology (Bachelard, 1992; Stewart, 1993; Kiendel, 2001), but they are too human-centered to work fully in an ANT context. Texts on different genres of miniatures are more numerous [1]. By looking at hobbyist activities on the net, Hine (2000) and Danet (2001) have made important contributions. Also to be mentioned are Belk (1995) on collecting – often deeply implicated in miniatures, Gelber (1999) on hobbies in general and Jackson et. al. (2000) on commercial culture, something that miniatures have been a part of to a high degree. But the main theoretical inspiration for this study of the networks of humans and non-humans comes from Bruno Latour, and models are in fact mentioned in his writings. In construction work models are often part of the design process, used both to develop ideas and to make them public. A recent anthology of ANT work contains several texts on this theme (Latour and Weibel, 2005). Addressing the fascination of models it is stated by one author that their importance does not lie in the difficulty in making them. Some models are made very fancy and with expensive materials, they may acquire the aura of an art object and become a sought after collector's object. But in the context of these Latourian writings, models are more interesting by showing at a certain moment in the process the many constraints that surround the development of the conception of a new building. The model is formed by all the actors that have expressed demands that went into it. A model that shows the surrounding city with roads and buildings, here is a material inscription that speaks of these constraints. The models discussed below both share something, and are different from the planning models of the design process. The difference is of course that the toy or the hobby miniature lacks any pretensions to serve as a planning device for a full-scale object. However both forms of models share an important trait in being formed as an outcome of contests of values and ideals

Miniatures in commercial culture

In the 19th century there was a revolution in color and form in the homes of the middle class brought about by printers and toy producers – card modeling and

[1] Dolls have been the subject of many studies (Peers, 2004; Rogers, 1998). Other topical studies concern ship modeling (Boyd, 2007), architectural models (Smith, 2004; Moon, 2005), card models of buildings (Nievergelt, 2001) or souvenir buildings (Majua and Weingarten, 1996), toy trains (Meyer and Damsch-Wiehager, 1988) or models as special effects in the film industry (Pinetau, 2005). Another approach to the subject of miniatures is work that addresses the mimetic characteristics of materials – paper (Pieske, 1984) wax (Bloom, 2003), plastic (Barthes, 1997; Buttgereit, 2000; Ward, 1999) or rubber (Bloor and Sinclair, 2004). Writings about card modeling and other paper crafts are voluminous in Germany, see for example Pieske (1984) or Stölting (1989). An online presentation of paper crafts by a competent author is *www.bildrum.se* (Sillén, 2007).

paper dolls were two paper technologies that reached wide circulation, sometimes as commodities, but they were also important factors in the commercial culture as promotions (Pieske, 1987). The cut-outs of cereal boxes in the sixties have many fore runners. Miniatures are part of commercial culture not just by being commodities; it is after all through miniatures (toys) that we all get enrolled into consumer culture. Also historically, miniatures as luxury goods were crucial in the process of developing the taste for consumption (Belk, 1995). To take the paper dolls as an example, they not just showed fashion, they also served as promotional gifts from a certain manufacturer. Paper dolls have closely followed the development of consumer capitalism. When dolls of pewter and wax kept their exclusivity, paper dolls reached the mass market. In the United States, paper dolls were often rallied to sell goods like Aunt Jemima's Pancake Flour or Enamiline Stove Polish. Singer sewing machines, Lyon's coffee and Clarke's threads are other examples of products that were sold by using the popularity of paper dolls. During the 30s to the 50s companies began to publish them in magazines. Sometimes the doll was printed right on the package of the product, sometimes it was delivered by post in exchange for a number of coupons.

The older forms of paper dolls and paper modeling depended on industrialized printing, making the technology restricted to the large numbers of mass production. In order to pay for the costly preparation of the lithographic stone, long series were necessary. Dolls, miniature buildings or ship models of paper that were turned out by the market leader J.F.Schreiber of Esslingen, Germany, or Pellerin of Epinal, France, had to stick to popular subjects to sell, adding a stereotypical restriction to the subject matter (Nivergelt, 2001). From an ANT perspective, not just authoritarian parents were limiting the choice for demanding children; the technology had the same aspiration to produce many cheap copies of the same thing. Moving on to the paper crafts of the web, the dynamic is significantly different. Sidestepping the expensive lithographic stone, thousands of computer terminals with printers provide the technological plumbing of modeling worlds that are highly fragmented. Many more different topics are treated, and many more ideals are made public through objects, as will be shown below.

Doing a Netnography

A couple of years ago he wanted to make a castle for his nephew. "I started with Google, typing *castle, paper* and immediately I entered a universe. I was

The London shop of designer Paul Smith is a typical promotional give away on the Japanese homepage of this firm. Photographer: Magnus Mörck

truly astonished realizing this – the great number of sites and people. But the Internet always does this, you write a word and a universe opens up." A male Italian civil servant, oceanographer at the research station in Trieste and known online as Paperpino, this prolific constructor of paper automata, is sitting by his country villa and tells about how he discovered his interest, his enrollment into the network.

I saw forums of discussion and I followed discussions, sites, online shops and then I also found a castle. The first model I downloaded was a simple car in black and white. And then I got started. Some sites gave a warning: Be careful, paper modeling is addictive. I never stopped from that time. Yes, that is it. I am lucky because my wife is very understanding and she is very nice and gentle because every night I build for two to four hours.

The following is an outline of the main web technologies that are important factors in the background of the above quote, resources for coupling new members onto the network of paper modeling.

- *Webpages* offer text and pictures and downloads with files from designers. Included are instructions for assembly. Some are to be paid for with a credit card or Pay Pal, but most are free gifts. The ones behind these sites are usually individual designers/hobbyists, but downloads are also supplied by corporations as promotional gifts. There are many different communities represented, educational institutions and state authorities. Webpages represent the most commonly used source of the project, including many hundreds.
- *Web rings* are made up by a number of webpages that have been linked in a certain order. They offer surfing around a theme and play an important role in the study, since they show what sites are considered as members of the hobby, for example those that qualify for The Paper Doll Web Ring.
- *Webzines* are electronic magazines that distribute information and documents on a regular basis. Only a handful of these were in existence during the time of the project.
- *News groups* are places where information is exchanged and members communicate in threads around topics of interest. This is the most organized level of activity, requiring a lot of work from the moderator and discipline from the members to keep away from controversial topics or straying away from the hobby. A few news groups were followed in the study, three of them based in U.S.A. and two in Germany. In web communities like this not only ongoing mail exchanges can be read, groups can also be provided with a memory through the storage of old postings.
- *Portals* serve as doorways leading to parts of the web that have been arranged thematically. In the project several webpages were found, ones that specialize in keeping track of and displaying links to other web pages with the same interest. In paper modeling there were three sites that had collected more than 400 links, one in Holland, one in USA and one in Taiwan. To share links of paper dolls there were a number of smaller collections and one large web ring.

Most downloads of paper miniatures originate in Western Europe and the U.S.A., but they are almost as numerous in East Asia – including Japan, South Korea and Taiwan. These are countries with a vital tradition in the paper crafts, for example origami. The eastern designers generally strive towards simpler and more original solutions than in the west. A much larger share of the output emanates from corporations and institutions – police, fire departments and public transport turning out unending lines of buses and vehicles.

When the hobbyists seek confirmation from each other, models are photographed and uploaded in albums or attached to ordinary e-mails. The album is an old technology that complemented amateur photography and has proved successful in adapting to the online environment, images are perfect for showing on monitors, and a click brings forth the next one, album pages with thumbnails providing order (Kitzman, 2004). The pictures studied proved to be subtly contextualized, placing miniatures of large scale objects like space ships, Middle Age German castles or racing cars in the sofa or on the kitchen table. This genre of self visualization on the net leaked domesticity brought about by direct visual links between different homes in Europe, the U.S.A., but also in many cases Japan and Taiwan. Images of models of instantly recognizable large-scale technologies communicated geographically diverse (often but not always) masculine interests in artifacts too huge and expensive for the individual to acquire, making up a space of technological artifacts that slipped through the barriers of language.

One of the main results of the appearance of the internet was diversification; many more people produced cut-outs or paper dolls than previously. In his home in Zoetermeer in the Netherlands, the architect Peter Visser, host of one of the largest lists of links, describes the change.

> I think the real thing that changed it was when I started to use a computer for designing; the first computers were not very suitable for making drawings. My first models designed on computer were just made ten years ago. That made things much easier, because for instance in the scale buildings, there are many windows that are exactly the same. I had to draw them all by hand and now all I have to do is just copy and paste and it is done. And when you make architectural models you get the plan from the architects and can use it for making the paper model. So that also makes it easier. It requires much less time than before.

The time-space of the activities have become, hardly global, but spread over several continents. An assemblage of producers, traders and consumer-collectors has formed. The ethnography traced the network from node to node, to see how humans and technology interact to produce outcomes; different genres of models evolve and these genres in turn influence which humans are recruited to the network, and the properties of the technologies enabling them, mediating between culture and technology, culture and economy.

> Yes, there are people who have always built paper models, now they design paper models themselves. With a computer it is much easier. When I designed my postcards fifteen years ago I had to draw them and go to the copy shop to make copies and then build them, make adjustments, and back to the copy shop. It took days, just going back for some simple postcards. With the computer and the printer I can do it in a few

> hours so it is much easier to do. A lot of people on the Internet design paper models, sometimes they are very good. And sometimes they are very bad.

Online there appeared a world of abundance and gifts became a favored way of building a reputation that could later be translated into jobs or commissions – attitudes closely related to the Open Source movement (Bergquist and Ljungberg, 2001). The celebration of gift-giving implied no real anti-market attitude, many designers started in a cottage industry of paper design, happy to charge their price on Pay Pal. Interviewed in her home south of Copenhagen, Dorte M Nielsen, civil servant and designer of paper dolls explains:

> The most important thing is to make something fun, but many times it is also important to know that there is a need for the dolls, that they can be sold. That means a lot, and for that reason I started the firm. I have the firm and I sell over the homepage, and also in some shops and museums. It is an important motivation, that somebody is interested in this; it is not enough to work for my own satisfaction, that's an important motivation.

From sky scrapers to the Universal Paper Doll

This section looks closer at some examples of paper crafts on the web, what kind of artifacts get around, what is the visual appeal of the 'free downloads' put on numerous webpages to arouse the appetites of innocent surfers – in order to enroll them into the network? Arguably one of the largest objects is a sky scraper designed by Frank Lloyd Wright, the famous architect, rising five hundred and twenty eight floors. It was never built, and no building anywhere stands more than half the height of this giant. But a handy one-meter model, scale 1/1700, of this construction can be downloaded from the homepage of Ralph Currell, a computer designer of U.K. In terms of assemblages and translations, to reach the data files you only have to type his address and move to the download page. As the PDF opens with ten pages you see all the parts that form the building, including white tabs where the pieces can be glued together. The whole construction is ready to appear fully in three dimensions, provided you have enough of the fourth dimension: time to spare for the exciting or boring process of assembling it. A gallery on the site shows previously published models through pictures uploaded by people who have succeeded in assembling them. In terms of materiality and translation this is really complicated, what was once an idea in the head of the famous architect has been deconstructed into pieces for printing in any terminal equipped with a printer. The idea wanders to a computer drawing, to a file reachable from any part of the net, is turned into print and paper, then assembled and photographed, the picture being uploaded to the site of Ralf Currell – appearing to confirm that teleportation finally is in fact possible. It is not of Star Trek capacity, but as long as it is made from paper, reasonably complicated models can be deconstructed and freely distributed anywhere. On his homepage the designers writes:

> Card modeling has always had a devoted following. Recently, however, interest in card models has increased worldwide due to the advent of the home computer and the Internet. Not only can card modelers from around the globe now exchange ideas, but in many cases the models themselves can be obtained in the form of a computer file, and be printed at home on a low-cost printer. Many companies and individuals are now selling or freely offering kits in digital form, and a new generation of designers is creating models using computer-aided-design programs.

The giant sky scraper is a vessel that serves to store an ideal, the reverence for a famous architect, a key figure in the modernist canon. Few downloads share this connection to high culture. In general they celebrate anonymous technology in any of its many appearances, whether a copy of a famous World War II RAF fighter, a satellite from NASA or a new car from Toyota.

Looking at the many thousands of paper dolls that can be found on the web, most serve to idealize common ideals of cuteness and elegance. P.J's Universal Paper Dolls offer seven different business suits for its female role figure and a large number of other clothes, skin colors and hair styles. Different from the gifts on the technological web pages, there is still a striking similarity with the cars and airplanes offered in many variations. Collecting is a theme close at hand and the virtuality of the net promotes this desire for numbers and minute variations (Belk, 1995). But not everything is order and numbers in this world of dolls and models. The Nazli and Kaan doll project from Turkey serves as a carrier of valuable information to the public on the family law reform of 2002, casting the girl with career aspirations in the airlines, the boy as a dancer. Janet Sue Terry's Fat Paper Dolls project great lives for round women, contradicting all stereotypical expectations. There is also a disabled doll from Gail's Paper Dolls with many wheelchairs to choose from.

In a heavily retouched photo a woman turns to show her transparent fairy wings glistening in mellow light. On her webpage she is surrounded by eight buttons, decorated with flowers. As you click yourself through the pages of this site, Flowers of the Dead, a virtual herbarium, you find large botanical drawings of poisonous or intoxicating plants. It looks pretty, but a bit dangerous. Behind the flowers paper dolls are hidden, one for each flower. Their dresses all come as variations of Goth fashion, looking trashy and sexy. Long texts ex-

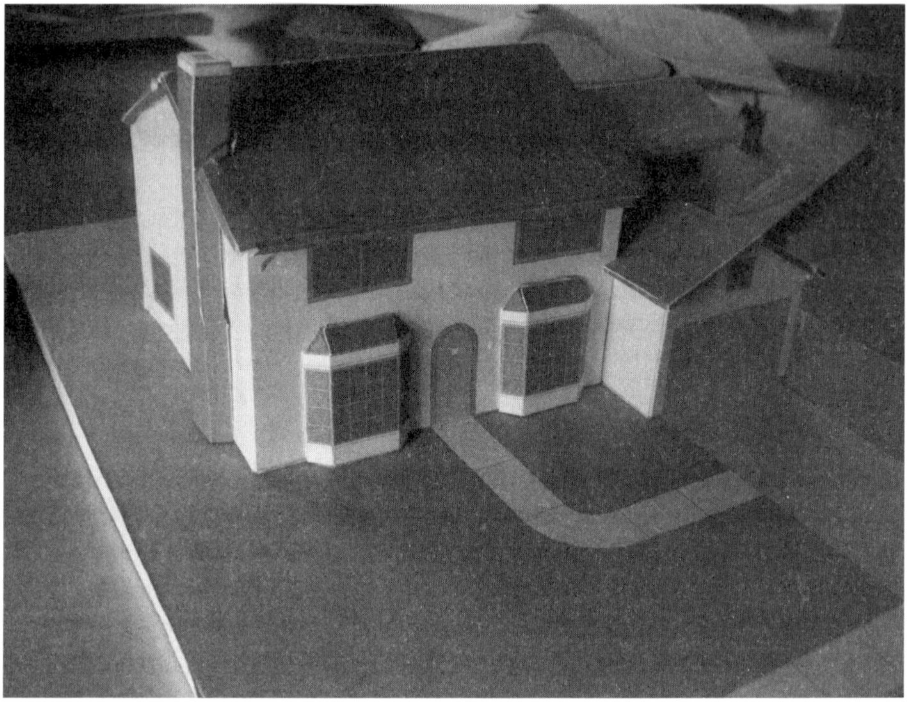

This Bart Simpson's house for free on an unofficial site is an example of paper models emanating from the many fan cultures on the internet. Photographer: Magnus Mörck

plain the flowers, like the poppy used for extracting opium. Poppy is of course also the name of that girl with Asian characteristics and her numerous dresses are presented with words like *Sleep, my bane*. Other parts of this voluminous site show the artist who has designed it all posing for pictures by a photographer friend. In a long series of carefully staged scenes she pulls a mummy out of a pyramid mausoleum. The mood is ironic; there is nothing really scary although the designer constantly refers to gothic iconography – like the table of contents that have the form of an opened carcass, pulling its breast open with different organs, clicking onto the pages of the site.

Somewhere you find the credentials of this female web designer, a list of the computer programs she masters – vital information to make public if you are looking for a job. There are also links to a number of firms and art projects that she has served. Among the customers are a small brand of designer clothes, a career consulting doctor, an Armenian film foundation and a local authorized car dealer in California. Flowers of the Dead is an interesting example of imaginative web design. The dolls are offered for free – you only have to pay for the ink and paper in case you want to print them out and use them. The site contributes to the status and personal aura of its heroine within the Goth subculture where she is well-known. At the same time it offers services in web design, complete with a price list. This way the gifts take part in a commercial venture. The dolls are new, but this combination of promotional gifts and the marketing of a product is part of an old package. There is a commercial circuit where the artist displays her skills to get customers. It intersects with the Goth subculture that provides much of the style and content of the work. Also there are links to other sites constituting a veritable rhizome of paper dolls.

The paper dolls on the Internet articulate many different cultural categories like gender, ethnicity or sexuality. They relate intimately to a value like hedonism as their most important interest is to change clothes. Age categories also get mixed up in the doll world in a way that is characteristic of our time (Lee, 2001). Dolls are for children, but in actual fact they are mostly chosen by their mothers. Children sometimes appropriate these artifacts, but basically they constitute the materialized desires of mothers. The dolls are mainly gifts circulating inside networks of women who are in their fifties. This adds a bizarre touch to this genre of visual culture of fashion dolls. The designers seldom seem to show a deep interest in what goes on in the fashion world at the moment, preferring to pull costumes out of a fantasy closet that holds dresses from few decades ago. The many glamorous dresses appear to be influenced by Hollywood star fashion of the forties or fifties. The paper doll world of the net is not contemporary in orientation. A basic sentiment is nostalgia. Most of the sites that belong to the paper doll web ring Auntie.dot.com look very nice and appropriate. They are the inheritors of a heritage of confining gender roles and restrictive femininity. As shown by the discussion of the Flowers of the Dead this is changing. However, this is not the only challenge for the old-fashioned doll. Pornography is a main player on the net and contributes to the paper doll world by portraying images of dolls as young girls getting violated in innumerable ways, or animated dolls that are undressed by a click on the mouse. But it is difficult to draw the line between images that subvert confining norms and those that harm in new ways for the benefit of the male gaze. That is the predictable moral confusion caused by the highly visible contestation of the paper doll on the net. Here we find the monster out of bounds, mixing dolls and online technologies regardless of conventional categorizations of child and adult content or male and female gazes. In the next section the ideals of the hobby will be shown once more, this time through its work ethic.

Magnus MÖRCK

The virtues of a hobby

To engage in the manufacture of models or miniatures during leisure time is to practice a hobby or a form of DIY, to use a concept that is broader and more recent. DIY is seldom highly evaluated in terms of skill or aesthetic quality, no doubt because there already exists artists, designers and crafts men who operate according to professional standards, blessed by established institutions. Instead of admiring its products, DIY has often been understood in a moral context, making it represent the successful infiltration of work ethic into leisure. Another source for the activities has been economic necessity; producing clothes, toys and decorating the home that otherwise were unaffordable. Steven Gelber (1999) has written the most thorough study of hobbies and focuses on their moral implications of self improvement. Hobbies were activities that started to appear during the 19th Century, with a strong emphasis on making men of middle-class families more adapted to home and family, to pull them away from public concerns and entertainment. Stamp collecting, carpentry or the collecting or manufacturing of miniatures involving male activities – toy soldiers, model railroads or ships – were activities that were promoted for keeping men at home and also in order to present themselves as good fathers to their sons. In hobbyism there is an overflow of industrial work ethic, the time for leisure and consumption is spent under the spell of work ethic. Patience and precision are key ideals to many hobbyists, as can be witnessed in the following interview extract.

Some people seem to like to make very small things.

Yes.

And that it is a value that you should be careful with – small things. I don't know, but you are not so attracted to the details?

No. I had a discussion a couple of years ago with Roger Pattenden, an English designer who makes Shakespeare houses, and he decided that the maximum number of parts for a model is 100. If you get to one hundred it is really too much. I don't like spending two months on one model very much, (...) it should take no longer than two days. Some people spend years on the large ships.

Why is that, do you think? What's the point in putting so much into one object, like building the Bismarck for three years?

If you do it well the result is really amazing.

You think so too?

Yes, I admire those people that have the patience to work on that kind of thing. I think I am a little too restless and think it would take too much time.

But it could also be a question of artistic or expressiveness or like... If you paint like Van Gogh, there are not too many details, but perhaps more emotion?

Yes. Now I have nothing to do with ships, so I am not tempted to build such ships, that is also a reason and buildings usually have fewer parts, because they don't have all the tiny boats and the cannons. The Titanic for instance, has all those little boats; you have to make dozens of the exact same thing.

Ideals work to inspire by pointing to levels of ambitions that are above the average, they create community and social cohesion, but they also tend to need care; being nebulous and fragile they are in need of protection. Grant McCracken (1988) argues that artifacts can serve as safety storage for ideals. By attaching ideas or norms to matter, the relative stability of the artifact will support the belief in the permanence of the idea. The ideal, which may be tricky and ambiguous, perhaps even dangerous, will be possible to handle, to be transported along great distances, be displayed in public for reverence or put away, buried underground in a safety storage for future use. Things work as objectifications of the ideas of humans and miniatures are perhaps especially well adapted to this purpose. Being reduced in size, miniatures puncture ordinary space, turn humans into giants and deprive them of their ordinary forms of physical agency. Susan Stewart (1993) writes about the doll's house that you cannot enter; it can only be consumed at a distance. This deprivation of agency comes with an excess of power: by being a giant you become free to smash the miniature. A combination of too much and too little agency marks the miniature out as a special case of materiality and visuality, a zone fit for fickle ideals. The above quoted authors, McCracken and Stewart, get some of the drama of humans interacting with miniatures, but do these writings correspond with an ANT theoretical frame? At heart they are perhaps too human-centered, ignoring the way things combine with humans to produce new configurations, not just being the objects of human will.

Moving from scale as a question of faithful miniaturization in an individual object, now let's look at comparisons between different objects. If you put many different objects of the same family in a relevant series like a timeline, something that can be taken for knowledge is created, a chain of development. Making the miniatures to a constant scale makes further comparisons possible.

The ghost train in Hayao Miyazaki's anime "Sprited Away" (2001) is celebrated in this piece of fan art from the net. Photographer: Magnus Mörck

Amassing many pieces of doll house furniture, alternatively paper ships makes for not just a collection but an environment with a comparative logic. When many hobbyists stick to one scale their world appears more tight and developed, all contribute to a given world of a certain size. Comparisons are a pedagogical strategy, knowledge and drama is created out of measurements. Certain questions are possible to answer instantaneously, is A larger than B? Power and performance in artifacts is fore grounded. In a study of modernist design Meikle (1995) points to the disruptive qualities of real-life technologies, they appear unexpectedly and instill both hopes and fears, old competencies and organizations get debunked, and new careers are made. By arranging lines of development among technological exemplars the chock is cushioned – models of course being the privileged medium for showing technologies slowly growing and changing like objects of nature. Models displayed together imitate the museum, suggests the comforts of evolutionary thought and recalls the prestige of scientific thinking. Here we find the monster of miniatures struggling for acceptance in the adult world, trying to appear dead serious, distancing itself from the children's room. Accuracy in handling scale and detail is an ideal among some modelers that fires prestige and ambition. Matt Bergstrom of Chicago interviewed on the ground floor of Aon building where he works at Dell in advertising.

Matt Bergstrom of Chicago designed this WTC memorial for downloading in scale 1:4000. Photographer: Magnus Mörck

There are some more World Trade Centers that you can download, have you seen them?

I have seen those, and I have made one of them and I have the same reaction as with other models: This isn't right! This is... I counted the floors and they were not the right number. One of the ones that I downloaded, I counted the number of windows across, and that was not correct either. I started out; I downloaded models and very quickly got the impression that I can do better than this!

The Aon building with the right number of windows can be downloaded from Bergstrom's homepage Build your own Chicago.

A Material Culture of Paper Crafts

Paper modeling means turning everything into paper, a material translation process is at the heart of this practice. Interviewed in Berlin, the architect Cord

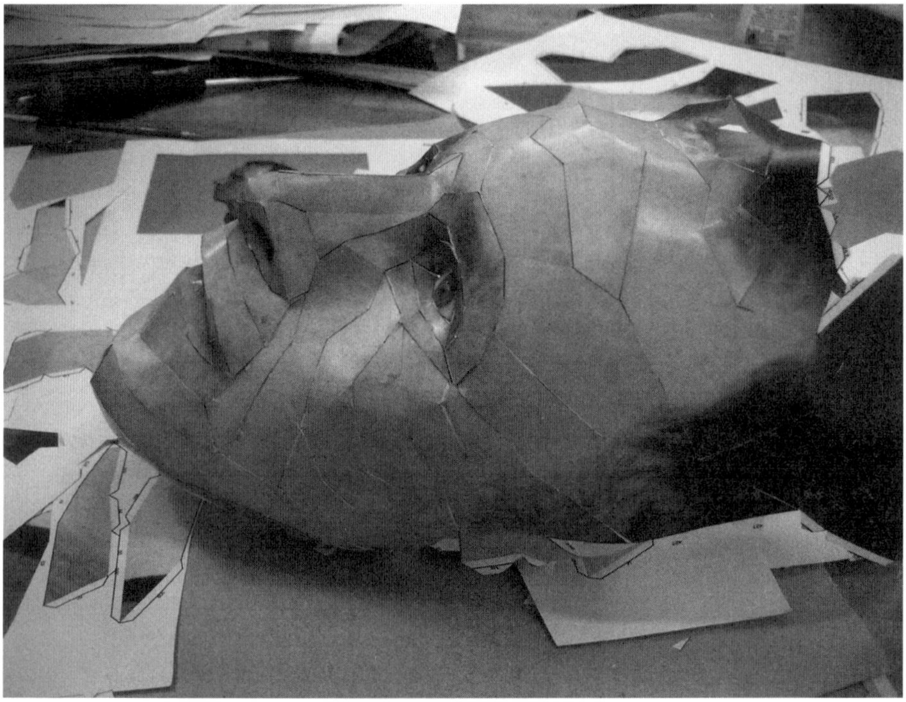

Bob Simmon's head downloaded from his site in data files. The two hundred parts are being assembled. Photographer: Magnus Mörck

Woywodt, designer of a line of models of iconic DDR architecture, makes a joke about how he does careful research on a building that interests him. 'And then you turn it into the opposite of what it is', from steel, concrete and bricks to paper. Any form of miniaturization brings up questions about translation of matter, details have to be discarded and ways of construction that are logical in full-scale buildings have to be exchanged. Here the modelers communicate with each other through the material –which is far from lacking in agency. Paper works well for certain shapes, like cubes or cylinders. Rounded objects and organic forms do not reproduce well. This might be the reason for this genre of modeling to prefer architecture and maritime topics to animals or human creatures. Paper models are printed and this means that they keep many traces of having been pictures, for instance there are often outlines in black print. Colors tend to be clear and the paper is seldom weathered for realistic effects of dirt or rust since it is technically difficult. These material properties contribute to the visual outlook of the objects. The iconography is materially determined or at least affected, the objects getting an idealized look, bright and optimistic in mood.

The forms of production also enter the process of material translation. Models are *hand crafted* artifacts, small representations of technological objects that in the original are manufactured industrially. Along with other forms of handicrafts, model building derives some of its value by sticking to forms of production that are in fact dying out. This is a theme that has been developed by Stewart (1993). Craft work is the original work process that was replaced by industrialism. In modeling typical machine-manufactured artifacts are made by hand. It is not so easy to see the meaning of this; many different interpretations could be made. Stewart puts the emphasis on nostalgia. We live in an industrial society, so people making hand-made objects are strange and trying to get away from the inevitable and this is a circumstance that adds fascination to card modeling. To make metal models of metal objects or paper models of paper artifacts would not have this particular twist in translating materiality. Paper models of ships are fascinating for many reasons – for instance by depicting ships that are of particular interest. But there is an underlying fascination in the whole genre that has to do with the contrast between real technologies and what they endure and paper, an extremely ephemeral material.

Miniatures and ambivalence

The next section moves into the territory of psychology, so beware. Although emotions are hardly lacking in the work of Latour, the ANT bent of the present analysis seems to prohibit psychologyzation. What does that mean? Narratives of human becoming are part of our monster, so without surrendering to psychology, let us say that schemes of developmental psychology are important to adult humans relating to miniatures. To some of the interviewed hobbyists and designers, it seemed important to distance themselves from modeling which implies childishness. This uneasiness stems from two sources, either it has to do with this activity as being seen as undignified and too simple to an adult or it has to do with perceived psychological schemes. The Danish doll designer Dorte M. Nielsen says that dropping the hobby was perfectly natural in her late teens. Only at the age of forty was it again possible to approach this area with confidence. Cutting off the childhood bonds to the monster of miniatures is sometimes an important part of making the alleged maturity of the individual public.

Let's take a closer look here, for some hot stuff. One main effect of miniatures is making us as humans become bigger; handling small things turns the child into a giant. Writing on 'the boyhood pleasure culture of war', Graham Dawson (1994) recollects feelings of omnipotence when handling small figures of soldiers. The intense feeling of rage when playing war is psychologically interpreted as a compensation for his lack of power in the hierarchy of the family. Growing up in Britain in the fifties, the World War II provided a main theme for boyhood play, with narratives from comics and television and miniature soldiers to act them out. He sees a double function of this war play: connecting to overarching public cultural values of the period where the recently ended war supplied material for masculine fantasies of identity, and a more individual drama of living out the frustrations of his family. In Dawson's narrative the war play materialized through miniature soldiers also becomes a powerful way of achieving masculinity through the suppression of domesticity, a way of withdrawing from the female part of the family. This topic is still highly charged to the author: he notes the similarities between the pleasure felt as a child in courting destruction, and the revulsion over these feelings coming later. Here there seems to be a theme that sometimes recurs in stories about adult's dealings with miniature worlds. There is a strong ambivalence about these artifacts of childhood, perhaps suggesting forbidden pleasures or threatening the adult with loss of control before consumer indulgencies. In the literature on dolls these uneasy feelings are readily apparent and often join the negative attitudes about fashion that were nurtured in a second wave feminism and tend to cast dolls as culprits of oppressive ideals. (Rogers, 1998; Peers, 2004). As exaggerated attributes of gender, pretty dolls and small soldiers seem well-suited for the excess of protestant guilt. Here the appetizing monster has lost all its charms. Please remove this embarrassing creature.

Modernism meant a cult of size; bigger was better, just think of sky scrapers, ocean liners, nuclear bombs, and giant corporations, super models in fashion and block-buster novels. The paper model world copies and recycles these giants of modernism. Models of ships and airplanes is a way of making these prestigious objects available, bringing them home, but this consumption is also subtly subverting the power of technology. The crisis of large-scale technologies, and of their gendered support in the ideals of masculinity spills over into doubts about a pastime, that covets the key symbols of the technological society. When the technologies are miniaturized and turned into flimsy paper,

Carnival glamour figure from Brazil – a promotional gift from Canon to boost the consumption of the printing ink produced by the company. Photographer: Magnus Mörck

is this a process of celebration or emasculation? Considering its charged subject matter, technologies and bodies, emotional ambivalence around miniature objects is not surprising.

The handling of printable downloads is fusing online and offline practice. The choice of method for the study, combining netnography with ethnography of the home drew attention to ideas and objects moving both ways (Lally, 2002; Mörck, 2006). The process in itself seemed to carry a cultural effect, a musing on the dematerialization entailed by digitalization and the Internet, a highly charged exercise in re-materialization, turning out an immense array of large-scale artifacts, available for free, where ordinary matter took on some of the infinite reproducibility of the digital media. Compared to Brenda Danet's (2001) pioneering study of net crafts the printables seemed to prove ambivalence towards dematerialization. Perhaps the age of the designers and hobbyists was crucial: most, both men and women seemed to be older than computer nerds in general. Using the computer to distribute and admire paper artifacts may have been a compromise, the digital tools are used as a means, but rejected at the end of the work process, here a real object was preferred, a boat, a doll or a house – not a virtual representation. At the same time the hobbyists seemed intensely social – a sociality that was directed towards the net. To collect admiration or advice from fellow hobbyists turned out to be an online affair.

Conclusion

The monster of printable downloads has revived paper crafts that were all but erased in the competition from plastic toys – both dolls and miniatures. Translated online the paper crafts appropriated the logic of distribution prevalent on the net. Two enthusiasms merged into one: the diligence of the hobbyist met the generosity of Open source – although there is always something expected in return for the gift. This chapter has explored how miniaturization worked to facilitate enrollment to the network. The network exploited and translated many of the resources found online: news groups, homepages and PDF files for secure distribution of image files or Pay Pal for net trade. Many different forms of social bodies flourished and contributed to a supportive environment: individual hobbyists and designers, net traders and corporations and institutions posting models and dolls as promotions. Certain topics were popular; technologies like cars or airplanes that the hobbyists had met in childhood reappeared and traveled easily across language borders. These artifacts had to be miniaturized in order to circulate; that is the practical reason of making models. But by using a material culture approach and borrowing thoughts from the phenomenology of small scale of Susan Stewart, it was demonstrated that miniaturization in itself was an attraction, a source of fascination. By being vehicles of disrupting ordinary space, miniatures attracted attention and contributed to the growth of the monster. But this power to enroll through fascination also entailed the opening up areas of ambivalence and insecurity: being too close to childhood memories and the powerlessness of childhood, miniatures also generate unease, a limiting factor in the growth of our monster.

II

Monster Playgrounds

Setting the Example – Building Privileged Trajectories in Interior Decoration Stores

Maria BRODIN

Music pours from invisible speakers. The warm dry air smells of coffee from the next-door café. My shoes, wet from the rain outside, add to the many footprints forming trails on the wooden floors. Glass walls and tapestry sections in white and light gray frame the large rectangular store. A large cash counter is situated at the very center. Around it white tables and shelves display a multitude of items. They appear organized according to living quarters; kitchen appliances, home office supplies, bathroom and cleaning items and the hallway interior. Colors, shapes and materials together with logos form different arrangements inviting visitors to look at and touch the items.

Two employees are busy unpacking newly arrived goods and putting them on display; another one is tending to a customer. Other people enter and exit the locale adding to the repetitive movement pattern of customers: entering, circulating tables, pausing for a moment, picking up and examining an item, looking for a price tag, replacing the item and moving on. After twenty-some years of being molded into a customer I too participate in this choreography of the store.

I follow a stream of people walking up to the second floor displaying fully furnished showrooms. Walls, textiles and wallpaper sections are used to arrange rooms displaying a variety of interiors. Three living room environments are followed by dinner tables and bedroom interiors. One of the living rooms features a large sofa in thick white fabric, a black and white striped wool carpet, a metallic lamp, a foot stool and a small black coffee table. Another one displays a sleek gray woolen sofa, an armchair in the same material, color and shape and a wooden coffee table. An off-white rya rug brings the items together. The third living room is undergoing some sort of rearrangement. It features the same combination of items but in a slightly different order. A wall with half-finished wallpaper. Rugs and pillows piled over a coffee table. An armchair has its back turned to its sofa.

Ordered on either side of a path, these full-scale arrangements alter the movement patterns of customers. No longer able to circulate the displays customers have to remain outside looking in or move into them, in a way becoming part of the display themselves. Sufficient examination of the items demand another set of movements; picking up is replaced by sitting down.

On one of the coffee tables I find a copy of the store catalogue. The two sites, the catalogue and the store mirror each other. An arrangement of glasses, vases, candlesticks, cutlery, pottery, hangers and coasters, sofas, tables, chairs, bookshelves, pillows, lamps and carpets; ordered and put on display.

But the items and orders displayed by the store and catalogue can be found in other places too. I have seen most of them before; in commercials, magazines, at cafés, and in the homes of my friends. All these sites display the same items and resonate the same orders. If a furniture store includes the same items as a home, arranged in similar manners one might ask what makes these places different. Where do the market end and the home begin?

The market/home divide

In this chapter I will discuss one of the many distinctions upheld by modern thought – the division between market and home. Positioned at opposite ends of a number of binary oppositions such as public/private, production/consumption and industrial/domestic market and home are concepts denoting locations as well as actions perceived of as separate. *Market* is a concept referring to an area or arena in which commercial dealings are conducted. It is a site where commodities are purchased and sold. *Home* on the other hand refers to an area of dwelling and nourishment. It refers to sites where people live permanently or locations of origin and growth.

Enacted in objects, the concepts of market and home translate into stores and dwellings; places that provide settings in which people as well as objects are ascribed with different qualities. In the store, people become customers or employees and objects become merchandise to be exchanged for money. In contrast, dwellings have been described a 'market place correctors' able to cleanse possessions from commercially assigned meanings (McCracken 1989). Here, both objects and people become members of a familial community maintained through affection and love.

However, during the last twenty years an exceptional increase in the 'homemaking market' has made retail and consumption practices fundamental to the way people organize, use and perceive their dwellings. Interior decoration stores, like the one accounted for above, are common features of contemporary life in Sweden. Together with catalogues, ads, interior decoration magazines and TV shows these places act as vehicles for contemporary ideals of home life (Clarke, 2001). Retail and promotion practice rely heavily on different techniques to assemble and distribute models of home environments. Conceptions of home are not only performed in people's dwellings but also to a large extent on the market. Following this, and due to their vast reach, commercial products are what make ideas of home and domesticity durable and distributed today.

Analogous, the market is becoming increasingly recognized as a vital ingredient of the most intimate parts of people's everyday lives (Arnould and Thompsson, 2005). For example, in the context of dwellings, commercial products and consumption are rendered important means for narrating identity (Marcoux, 2001; Reimer and Leslie, 2004) as well as relationships and love (Gregson, Metcalf, Crewe forthcoming). Recent writings on dwelling practices bring forward the repetitive work of negotiation and change required to maintain a harmonious relationship between the dwelling and identity narratives (e.g. Clarke, 2001; Gregson et al forthcoming; Reimer and Leslie, 2004). This way consumption, which connects market practice to non-commercial practices, has become a vital part of the conception of home.

The contemporary situation, where stores and other retail objects becomes central to how dwellings are organized and perceived, distort and raise questions about the divide separating market and home. Is it still possible to make the same distinction between market and home? Although the geographical separation remains – most people still live and go shopping at different locations – the commercialization of home life suggests a conceptual change. Therefore, a perhaps more relevant question is – in what way are the market and home connected and what implications does this connection have for contemporary understandings of home?

Purpose

The purpose of this chapter is to describe how 'home' is performed in interior decoration stores in order to discuss how conceptions of the market and home connect. Departing from an Actor-Network Theory (ANT) perspective I provide a tentative reading of interior decoration store practice and I discuss how the workings of the store rely on a continuous work of hybridization where market and home are performed simultaneously. Introducing the hybrid 'store-living room', I pay particular attention to how practices, which I call season-ing, styling, tagging and displaying participates in the performance.

Observations made in three different interior decoration stores during spring 2004 provide the empirical basis of this chapter. Besides observations of store locales, websites and catalogues also provide material for the discussion.

In the following section, I introduce a spatial perspective based on ANT that allows places such as interior decoration stores and dwellings to appear as performed and related to each other in networks. In contrast to previous research on stores, for example in the marketing discipline, where stores are portrayed as containers enclosing commercial dealings, this perspective renders stores as assemblies performed through the practice of these dealings. It makes visible how store places rely on operations of association rather than separation.

Next, utilizing this perspective, the spatial practices of the store are outlined through the example of the 'store-living room'. This example illustrates how notions of 'home' and 'market' are performed and blurred in the interior decoration store. In the last section I discuss implications of the store practice and argue that the store perform 'home' in a way making issues of time, style, interchangeability and the visual important to its conception.

Making connections

How are interior decoration stores and dwellings connected? Turning to previous research on stores and consumption in marketing (my discipline of origin), it becomes evident that this connectedness has not been accounted for. Rather, the conceptual and geographical divide between stores and other places in society, for example dwellings, is maintained within this field. One of the reasons for this is passive stance taken on space.

Contemporary marketing management research focusing on the retail environment derives from the conceptual framework of Servicescapes [1] (e.g. Bitner, 1992; Clarck and Schmit, 1995; Arnould, Price and Thierey, 1998; Sherry, 1998; Sharma and Stafford, 2000; Tombs, McCall and Kundery, 2003). Although the development of this literary field is an attempt to acknowledge and seriously examine the spatiality of retail practice, the vast majority of this research departs from a static and uncritical perception of these places (Ek, 2002). Although the interior of the store is described as open for manipulation

[1] In 1992 Mary Jo Bitner launched the concept Servicescape that formed a theoretical framework anchored in the tradition of environmental psychology where dimensions like ambience, spatial layout and symbolism were used to explore the behavioral impact of physical and spatial conditions on customers and employees (Bitner, 1992).

by managers, Servicescapes are still represented as natural mediums containing and isolating actions as well as actors. Stores become fixed spaces, i.e. inside them identities and orders are fixed and unable to escape the enclosure of the store. This way Servicescapes are associated with naturalness and intrinsic and autonomous qualities; they become narrated as a-political, a-cultural and a-historic places which prevent research from acknowledging the performance of these places (Ek, 2005).

In consumer research, another field of marketing research, efforts have been made to represent store milieus as contexts of consumption thereby underlining the mutual dependency between consumption practices and store places (e.g. Sherry, 1997; Sherry, 2000; Brown and Maclaren, 2005). Retail and consumption are recognized as taking place in and performing a physical environment, but still emphasis is placed on objects and meanings produced within the borders of the store locale rendering it as enclosed and contained. At the expense of relations between store and other places in society, the inquiry is dedicated to the interaction between store and consumer. Possible connections between stores and places 'outside' the store still remain undisclosed. In order to acknowledge the changing relation between market and home in contemporary Swedish society, a different outlook is needed.

A spatial perspective drawing on ANT makes visible workings that remain hidden in marketing discourse. Firstly, ANT underlines relationships and their distributions making space appear as a consequence of the production and reproduction of relationships (Law, 2000). It renders space (and time) as effects rather than conditions for events and action (Latour, 1997; Law, 2000; see also Lefebvre, 1995/1974; Thrift, 1996; Thrift, 2006). From this perspective reality and its orders are continually enacted rather then permanent. According to Bruno Latour (1997) there are no absolute stable spaces only more or less successful efforts made to make space appear stable. Therefore, secondly, as pointed out by Annemarie Mol (1999), ANT brings the *performance* of reality to the fore. The market is continually performed at different locations, for example in the interior decoration store. The same argument applies to the home, which is enacted in the store as well as in people's dwellings.

ANT brings forward the work done by marketing research. By representing the store as a stable entity constituted by fixed elements, marketing research participates in the performance of a *regional topology*. Regional topologies represent places as regions defined by boundaries performed through the suppression of differences inside a certain site (Mol and Law, 1994). By marginalizing the internal heterogeneity of a site, boundaries are performed in relation to other sites. For example, placing focus on practices and props of management and selling, the Servicescape concept creates regions of retail. Based on the occurrence of these elements a store appears delimited from other places, for example, an office or a dwelling. This way stores as well as the practices that perform these sites appear isolated and stable. Consequently, examining a place using a regional typology, no apparent connections between store and dwelling space are made visible and the market/home divide is maintained.

However, if a *network topology* is utilized a different picture emerges. A network topology does not exclude regional topologies (Mol and Law, 1994). But instead of setting boundaries between areas through the suppression of heterogeneity, network typology draws attention to heterogeneous elements and the way they hang together (Mol and Law, 1994). A network topology does not treat proximity as a question of here and there in metric terms. Instead proximity has to do with the identity of a semiotic pattern. A semiotic pattern is a combination of elements *ordered* in a manner that convey a certain meaning. Places with similar orders of elements and relations are close to one another while places with different orders are further apart. From this perspective interior decoration stores and dwellings could be described as close to one another since they display a similar semiotic pattern.

According to network typology, *connections* are made through *orders*. It points towards the *ordering* and *stabilizing* of work that lingers behind places. The question, then, becomes how are orders made? In a discussion on how place is performed, Kevin Hetherington (1997) elaborates on the ordering work involved in the process.

Hetherington emphasizes the importance of acknowledging the events and actions that make places appear. He argues that places are mobile arrangements generated through a process of:

- *Placing* materials in relation to each other, i.e. bringing them into connection or comparison, making them form an assemblage.
- *Arranging* those *placings* so that they can be known and represented through immutable mobiles, i.e. enabling them to fix and represent an order or arrangement as indisputable while allowing it to travel.
- *Naming* the arrangements, i.e. make them known as meaning something specific.

Imagine for example the following assemblage gathered from my opening account of the interior decoration store: *wooden floor*, *tables*, *shelves*, *coffee cups*, *towels*, *logos*, *lamps*, *carpets*, *barcodes*, *walls*, *hangers*, *people*, *loudspeakers*, *sofas*, *vases*, *armchair*, *wall paper*, *rug*. Placed in a row or a pile, these items make no immediate sense. The gathering of bodies would perform spatiality through their *placing*, but they would not perform place since their ordering would not convey any meaning in particular. [2] To perform a place the placing of the bodies has to be *arranged* in an order that affords actions central to the place in question.

Just like syntactical orders make me place nouns in relation to each other in a certain manner to produce my description of the store, the *practices* of retail such as displaying, selling and storing, produce gatherings of material, of physical bodies, that relate or connect to each other in a specific manner. The performance of place is therefore dependent on the ability of social practices to arrange placings in a manner particular enough to be known and recognized as part of some pattern or category. This way the *arranged placings* could also be made known as meaning something specific, i.e. they could be *named* in this case 'interior decoration store'.

Hetherington's model underlines the significance of practice. To understand the workings of a place attention should not only be directed towards the elements and orders that constitute place, but also to practices that assemble elements and constitute the orders. Orders are not 'natural or innate to a place. Instead, they are an effect of a continuous work of inclusion and exclusion.

By placing certain objects in relation to each other while demarcating them from other arrangements, practice generates orders. Also, through continuous work of performing and repeating an order practice makes them appear as common sense (Hetherington and Munro, 1997).

Another important aspect of Hetherington's model is his concern with ma terial and nonmaterial qualities of place. Practices as well as the orders and places they produce are constituted by material and nonmaterial elements. Hetherington uses the term *utopics* [3] to discuss the relationship between material and nonmaterial aspects of place.

Utopics is a spatial process of ordering and reordering where ideals and ideas are translated into material form. According to Hetherington (1997) all

2 Some readers might object to the argument that the nouns make no sense. In my text they do make sense but only through the context I provide them with. Contextualized differently for example on the first page of this book their appearance would be more confusing.

3 Utopics is a term developed by philosopher Louis Marin derived from a deconstructive reading of Thomas More's Utopia. According to Hetherington (1997) Marin's interest was directed towards the gap or the ambivalence created between the ou-topia (no place) and eu-topia (good place) that the original concept referred to. Marin used utopics to denote spatial processes of ordering and disordering trying to close this gap. Utopics is a spatial play on the theme of utopia.

places resonate a meaning and a name that derives from an ordering of arrangements that connotes to an ideal. The ideal of a specific place is in turn linked to the 'affordance' of that place.

For example, stores originate in a will to *exchange*. Through retail practice, i.e. the practice of selling this will is translated and materialized performing a place of flux and change. Exchange is the utopic of the store, a spatial play on the theme of mobility. In order to perform exchange stores are open and public. Customers are welcomed and a certain degree of anonymity is produced. A continuous flow of people as well as financial resources is needed to maintain the store.

In contrast, dwellings and homes originate in a will to *belong*. Many studies argue that dwellings and the items they consist of are material performances of identity and anchors of life narratives (e.g. Marcoux, 2001). Contrary to the store, homes are described as sites where comfort is attained and memories are stored. In this context change might even be considered hostile to the dwelling place (McCracken, 1989). The secluded quality of dwellings ensures privacy. It is a place that strives to create comfort thereby producing intimacy.

An interior decoration store and a dwelling rely on similar elements and the same process of placing, arranging and naming. Both feature similar objects – furniture, decoration and domestic utensils – but still they are perceived as places with different qualities. One of the reasons for this is that they are arranged differently, guided by different utopics. While the ideal of the store is to create endless exchange in order to maximize turnover, the ideal of the home is to create endless belonging in order to secure identity and comfort.

However, places are always monstrous. Impure and heterogeneous they rely on a myriad of connections and workings that rely on 'mismatched' orders. For example, to make exchange happen the interior decoration store rely on orders of home. Today, selling furniture and decoration items involve the practice of arranging and displaying the items according to orders of a dwelling, which is a translation of home into material form. In this sense the utopics of the interior decoration store is connected to the utopics of home – exchange is linked to belonging.

While a network typology make visible semiotic connections between interior decoration stores and dwellings Hetherington's model emphasize the importance of acknowledging the practices that make these connections. Therefore, in order to discuss how market and home are connected I need to examine practices as well as different orders as they unfold in the interior decoration store. To accomplish this I focus on one particular monster – the 'store-living room'. The 'store-living room' is an arrangement of heterogeneous materials brought into connection by store practices. In order to explain the performance and workings of the monster both elements and practices that connect them must be accounted for. In the next section I account for its orders, i.e. the placed and arranged elements the monster consist of. In the following section the different practices forming these orders are discussed.

The living room monster

Situated on the second floor of the interior decoration store, the 'store-living room' I use as an example here is one of many full-scale room displays. As one out of three living room environments it provides the first scenery customers encounter when entering the second floor. The display features a large three-seat sofa in thick white fabric and metallic legs. Its wide seat affords sitting as well as lying down. Pillows in the same color and material are placed on low armrests that could just as well function as headrests. A lean metallic lamp stands just beside one of them. The sofa faces a small rectangular black coffee table and a large footrest. Two candlesticks, an empty glass bowl and a rather small but still conspicuous purple sign with 'Spring News' in large white letters are placed on the table. The furniture is placed on a black and white striped wool carpet that connects them and makes them form a unit. Two walls, one in a black and white pattern and one in black frame the arrangement. Tags with varying information are attached to all the items. Some display only price and a barcode; others also entail information on measurements, materials and manufacturer. The smaller items, such as pillows and candlesticks, have alarm tags attached to them.

The perhaps most immediate qualities of the 'store-living room' are all these material elements that constitute it. Non-human bodies in different sizes and shapes provide it with its material form. But beside the different material elements such as pieces of furniture, decoration items and tags, the arrangement also entails a number of other elements; elements that are commonly described as non-material but still rely on materiality to take form and travel, namely ideas. They exist as postures, shapes or orders performed by material bodies.

Ideas on what a living room is, what it should look like and what activities it should afford play an important role here[4]. If items are not ordered in a

[4] Different contexts entail different ideas of what a living room is and what it should afford.

manner corresponding to these ideas, the arrangement does not perform the intended work. Following the logic embedded in retail practice, the 'store-living room' is intended to connect different products in order to provide a model. The idea is to put the products in a context – commercializing not just individual products but a concept of living. The arrangement categorizes the items according to the categories of a (Swedish) dwelling. They are no longer just a carpet or a lamp but a living room carpet and living room lamp.

However, the items are also living room carpet and lamp for sale. In addition the arrangement also performs the store. The 'store-living room' relies on ideas of retail store organization. Customers must recognize the arrangement as a living room environment, but also as a 'store-living room' environment. Ideas on what a store is, what it looks like and what it does are therefore just as important. For example, the display and pricing of items are important elements in the performance of the 'store-living room'. Anchored in retail and exchange practices these ideas secure the performance of the arrangement.

If the arrangement is misinterpreted – if it is taken for a home living room – it would not perform the intended work. Home living rooms, although including the same objects, afford a different set of movement pattern for both people and things. These places rely on different rhythms. While the store relies on choreography of moving around, browsing and mobilizing objects, the home living room follows another pattern of movement. Here object movement is more constrained; they are bound to these sites and typically to a set of people.

The 'store-living room' is a particular breed of monster made up of a mix of selling and dwelling orders. This particular combination of orders enables a fusion of the stable and familiar and the mobile and unfamiliar. It also makes the connection between homes and stores (markets) evident. But how and why are these connections made?

Assembling the monster – performing orders

The 'store-living room' is performed through a number of spatial practices anchored in retail and trade. These spatial practices, as they materialize the utopic of the store, consist of a number of events in which many different actants participate. Like the store the 'store-living room' is a spatial effect of a will to make objects exchangeable. How is this accomplished?

The 'store-living room described here adhere to ideas valid in a Swedish, early 21st century context. For a discussion on varying perceptions see for example Kragh & Djursaa (2001).

To make exchange happen objects have to be known and recognized as able to move. In this section I address four practices that perform the 'store-living room' as a mobile entity. The first practice I call *season-ing*, which denote actions that attribute the 'store-living room' with a specific temporality. The second practice *styling* involve efforts to portray the 'store-living room' as a specific set or genre while the third *tagging* concern methods for making its individual parts to appear as connected to assemblages outside the store. The last practice *displaying* concerns procedures that make the 'store-living room' a visual object.

Season-ing

The specific temporality of the interior decoration store is emphasized through practices like redecoration of show rooms and the introduction of items not previously displayed. In the 'store-living room' the sign 'spring news' lets customers know that items have not been for sale before thereby emphasizing the arrival of items. It also separates this particular arrangement from others not displaying this sign. The 'news' sign and its counterpart 'sale' are important instruments in the practice of ordering objects according to temporal categories. Other practices that support the performance of temporality are the release of catalogues and other promotional material.

These practices of redecoration, the use of news and sales signs and the distribution of promotion material support the temporality of the store. In retail practice this temporality have been labeled season and together with shorter cycles like opening hours they manage the flow of items and people passing through the store. Enacted through the spatial practices of the store temporality also provides a hierarchy since it is connected to value. New items receive a superior position in the hierarchy of things than for example items for sale, which are considered yesterday's news.

Styling

The second example, styling, operates in a similar manner. Style is performed through operations of inclusion and exclusion where items are assembled, arranged and labeled.

Besides the 'store-living room' described above, the interior decoration store features two additional living room environments. As accounted for in the opening of this chapter the the arrangements exhibits items of different color, patterning, material, and shape making them appear dissimilar. Although the effect primarily appears to be visual, differences are tactile as well. The model and material of furniture afford different body postures. A sofa tightly upholstered and one with more pliable down cushions provide different support for the body – style looks and feels different. Using a set combination of furniture in three environments and then adding different details, customers are educated and made aware of the importance of detail.

Style is also used to categorize and order items in the store catalogue. Besides visual illustration of different versions of, for example, the living room, arrangements are also described as different in texts supplementing the images. Text also provides the means for the use of labels and labeling. Labeling is a process where ideas are turned into linguistic artifacts through repetitive use of a label (Czarniawska and Joerges, 1996). Using different sets of adjectives (warm, relaxed, classic, daring, pure) and connecting different material with different values the interiors in the catalogue come across as different. A living room is not just a living room but also an expression of styles named for example 'Elegant', 'Urban' or 'Classic'. Through arrangements and use of words the store and its catalogue adhere to a process where words such as 'style' but also 'Elegant', 'Urban' or 'Classic' have become matters of course in the context of interior decoration. Through frequent repetition over time in magazines, TV shows, stores and catalogues these words have become quasi objects.

The spatial play of the store produce patterns, which are used to label items according to for example appearance and material. By ordering items according to styles the interior decoration store performs sets or series forming a distinctive appearance, design or arrangement. These sets work in two ways. First, they make individual items part of a set thereby generating opportunity and desire to complete the set. Second, sets also provide semiotic mobility, i.e. exchanging one or two of the items of an arrangement create a new set.

Tagging

In order to make exchange happen, objects have to be connected to networks enabling them to move and become transferable. [5] In the store these connections are made through a process where objects are translated into numbers.

[5] While some writings portray the exchange process of goods and money as a process of decoupling (Callon 1999), others advocate that exchange and mobility is generated through connections (Appadurai 1986). I align to this later position.

The tags attached to the items in the 'store-living room' are the most visible consequence of this practice.

Although seemingly common and modest, these tags attached to items through pins and glue, constitute a vast amount of compressed information. Their barcodes and number series entail information on an object's material qualities and position in different ordering and storage systems. When the items of the 'store-living room' enter the store they are carriers of numerous of connections. These tags bare witness of these connections making objects part of networks stretching far beyond the interior decoration store. Taking this argument one step further I argue that tags are actors; they provide a unified voice for the many humans and non-humans whose work they rely on. The numbers and codes on the tags of the 'store-living room' are a consequence of a long chain of valuation and negotiation between different actors in the commodity chain. Tags speak for the items they are attached to as well as the makers and distributors of that item. Through their voice the items receive a position in a value system – they are assigned a price.

In the store this position is supplemented with additional connections. Using a more or less standardized mark-up store practice positions items within a system of value. Printed on a tag and attached to an object the price indicates this position but it also creates a connection to customers. Tags speak of previous connections but they also signal the opportunity to make new ones. A price tag is also a vehicle making it possible to move an object from the store to another setting. It signals opportunity.

As all items in the 'store-living room' carry price tags they are possible parts of other environments. They are made into exchangeable attributes of a dwelling. Therefore, the spatial order of the store is also an enactment of making visible the possibility of moving items from the store to a home setting. Almost every costumer that enters the store has the possibility to acquire the items of the 'store-living room'. If customers do not have the necessary funds the store offer consumer credits.

Displaying

A fundamental practice of the store is to put merchandise on display. There are many different techniques of accomplishing this and the interior decoration store provides several examples. Things are put on shelves and tables, in display cases or on pedestals. Show rooms are created through the arrangement of walls and textiles. Regardless of the technique used, the intention is to make items visible. Items are made into objects to be looked at; they are made into visual entities.

The second floor of the store, where the 'store-living room' is situated, is organized in a manner that creates a spacious environment where customers are intended to walk a path passing the show rooms. The floor is organized to create a corridor of displays granting primacy to a visual logic. Customers can only try and feel the material of the furniture and decoration items by venturing from the path. In this way the 'store-living room' presents itself as a visual entity; as an image to be looked at and evaluated based on its appearance.

The spatial order of the 'store-living room' is an enactment of display and the gaze. Customers are encouraged to look at the displays and items as much as they want, while touching is restricted to occasional strokes, lifting or sitting down. Trying items out by using them is strictly forbidden. Using the 'store-living room' to read a book, sleep or have coffee with friends is not an option. Being a customer is a disciplining activity where vision is encouraged and the use of other senses discouraged.

Building a privileged trajectory

The 'store-living room' is not a passive and quiet entity but an active and sometimes even loud performer. Resonating domestic as well as retail orders, the 'store-living room' perform a particular concoction of belonging and exchange. It turns the gaze of customers towards their own living room environments, proclaiming that these places are similar but still different. Packaged and re-packaged through practices of seasoning, styling, tagging and display the 'store-living room' performs domesticity, but it is a domesticity made up of exchangeables and images characterized by seasonal temporality and style. In the 'store-living room' belonging is achieved through continuous change.

The 'store-living room' is one of many performances of 'home' today. A question such as 'what is home?' cannot be answered in one way as home is performed in several co-existing versions. It is neither conceptually nor geographically restricted to dwellings.

The example of the 'store-living room' illustrates how retail practice influences a particular home performance. Behind the orders of the 'store-living room' different practices unfold; practices that opens up for the possibility of inter-topological effects making the operational rules of one place interfere with those of another (Mol and Law, 1994). Through a significant impact on how home is performed and conceptualized in the interior decoration store, the utopics of the store interfere with the utopics of home.

Neatly packaged the 'store-living room' provides the double service of a model; it claim to represents a living room but at the same time it provides a mold for this particular environment. Besides affording retail and consumer practice, the 'store-living room' actively participates in the making of a privileged trajectory. Out of a vast number of possibilities it literally and figuratively builds a path – an order – organizing human as well as non-human elements.

For example, the 'store-living room' contributes to 'visualization', i.e. raising the status of sight over touch, taste, smell, and sound, which have been appointed as a distinctive feature of modernization (Cooper, 1997). Also, besides encouraging customers to look the 'store-living room' also suggests how to look. For example, in contrast to the spatial set up of charity shops where customers are required to find their own path and their own way to look (Gregson et al, 2002 at the merchandise) the interior decoration store quite powerfully suggests a way of looking. Here looking is managed and ordered through the spatial setup of showrooms and categories performed by practices like seasoning, styling and tagging.

This way the 'store-living room' performs a line of sight (Munro, 1997), a way of seeing and conceptualizing home. Like other places based on exhibition and display the interior decoration store construct a point of view (Hetherington, 1999). It performs geometry of seeing and ordering.

As the home is part of the store and the store a part of home the 'store-living room' makes store and home become subjects of the same hierarchies. Monsters like the 'store-living room' connects locations, which are located far from each other in metric terms. As the modern division between home and market starts to fade new divides start to appear. Public/private or anonymous/familial living rooms succumb to scales of new/old, well matched/unmatched, and exchangeable/non-exchangeable. Traditional ideas of domesticity are challenged and other ways to belong suggested. Through the spatial play of retail practice the 'store-living room' performs and names a place – a market home – against which other arrangements are positioned and calibrated.

To Consume and Be Consumed

Birthday Parties at McDonald's

Helene BREMBECK

'Is it the prince's or princess' birthday? A party at McDonald's is a way for you as a parent to put your child at the center without any reservations', the Swedish homepage entices when introducing the new theme birthday parties 'Princess and Knight' and 'Indians' in 2003. The regular Ronald McDonald party from the sixties with Ronald party hats, napkins, and balloons, and a visit to the kitchen seemed somewhat outdated at the turn of the new millennium. Now high hopes have come along with the new theme parties as experience raisers bringing McDonald's out of the crisis of decreasing sales and diminishing customer rates, that the company was facing, and here activities for children like birthday parties fit perfectly.

In this chapter the McDonald's birthday party will be narrated as an ordered relational event, a network emerging around the celebration of the child involving several actors and trajectories, where the affordance of the restaurant plays a vital part, and where certain 'monstrous', birthday personas are generated. The performance of place, discussed in depth in the previous chapter, has already started to take place: objects/bodies are arranged in a manner that afford actions central to the rationality of the restaurant-performing-a-party. The focus is instead on conducts and subjectivities – little monsters – generated by the party-net in action. Framing the party at the restaurant allows a bit of divergence from the standard recipe of Latour of 'starting in the middle and looking for connections' (1999), in that this event as well as the premises are already distinguishable from surrounding activities, they are already framed. To some extent the actors are also known, or at least we have a good idea of who some of them are (parents, presents, children, cake, staff). This, however, not only resonates well with Barbara Czarniawska's suggestion to focus on the action or happening (Czarniawska, 2004), and Mike Michael's urge to follow the hybrids (Michael, 2000), it is also a way of highlighting the power of the place/space, where this action unfolds, and the hybrids move. This is done with the help of the concept affordance.

Affordance, a concept clearly resembling the Latourian concept of prescription, has been elaborated by Mike Michael (2000) to capture the fact that

Johan at McDonalds's 2006. Photographer: Magnus Mörck.

surfaces and structures that make up a body's environment specify a range of possible actions for that body. The design of the restaurant, the party corner, the furniture etc. 'afford' or suggest certain actions – lying, sitting, standing, crawling, hopping, jumping – that mirror the body's corporeal capacities as well as current discourses of for example restaurant design, or of children's comportment in public spaces. Thereby they guide the party-actors; on the one hand closing down possible actions/paths, while at the same time making new connections and new paths possible that were not previously thought of, by for example the children, or parents. We will now take a trip to the Birch Grove McDrive situated close to one of the main roads approaching Göteborg, where I did fieldwork during the spring of 2003 [1]. There we will take a closer look

[1] The birthday party study was part of my subproject in the *Commercial Cultures* project, on McDonald's as a family ritual. I also collected data from the homepage of Swedish McDonald's, including the digital Happy Meal archive, made interviews with executives, marketers, staff and customers, visited suppliers and took part in other McDonald's activities, like the 'Happy Mil' (Happy Mile) – a running contest for children. The project as a whole is presented in the book *Hem till McDonald's* (Home to McDonald's) (Brembeck, 2007).

at the premises, where real-life performances of McDonald's birthday parties took place.

The monster playground

The Birch Grove McDonald's is a fairly large, rectangular building with large windows covering three of the outer walls. On one side of the road there are residential blocks of apartments and condominiums, and a bit further away terraced houses followed by bungalows. On the other side there are workplaces; small industrial buildings, warehouses, offices, and a small center with a gas station, a hotel and a few technical equipment stores. During the weekdays, the restaurant is primarily used as a place to have lunch for people working nearby, and as a place to grab a bite for taxi and lorry drivers passing by. Families with children appear on weekends, mostly mothers and fathers with one, two, or three children, but also lone fathers, or grandfathers bringing children for a weekend treat. The restaurant is transformed into a family restaurant, and it is then a place where the majority of children's birthday parties are held, although they are also offered on weekday evenings.

The main entrance is on one of the short sides, and when you enter you can easily detect the counter at the opposite wall, where the easy-to-grasp menu with words and colorful pictures hang above. Behind the counter there is the kitchen with storerooms, such as the big freezer, machines, and counters where the hamburgers are 'swung' in the inscribed way, lockers where the ready-made food is stored for the customers for a regulated couple of minutes, and then thrown away to avoid lack of freshness. In a separate booth close to the counter there is the serving hatch for the Drive-In customers. In the far back are facilities for the staff. The dining area is a large room with an inner region divided into several smaller parts by green plants and screens. The children's corner is at the right-side wall. Standing at the main entrance you have a good view of what is happening in most corners of the restaurant, while sitting down you can hide yourself among the green plants and easily find an undisturbed corner.

The affordance of the premises

The children's corner consists of two glassed-in rooms connected by a small open cloakroom and a white chain closing off the play area from the rest of the restaurant. The cloth hangers are adult-size, requiring adult assistance to reach, and thus prescribing the children as minors and the adults as the ones in charge. One of the adjacent rooms is as good as totally filled with a climbing frame in two floors, consisting of two plastic tubes that wind up to the second floor. On the upper floor the tubes level out to constitute huts. The tubes afford the children to climb, crawl, slide, and run upwards, and downwards, and to perform numerous little power tricks to hinder, or support the passage of the other children. The huts on top provide not only an escape from the ruffle in the tubes, but also a way to be in control, and to show off in front of adults, and children passing by outside. During my fieldwork the chain closing off the play area had a broken hook, and this was of a special importance, since it enabled other children to get into the play area, if not guarded. This chain with its broken hook invited a range of actions for the children; waving it – threateningly or invitingly – holding it high, walking around with it, and most of all trying to fasten it again, securing that no trespassing was made.

While the play room was not demarcated from the cloakroom, there was a door closing off the party room, that was shut when there was a party going on inside. The two glassed-in walls facing the dining area did not reach the ceiling but left a gap open at the top, which not only made the children visible from all over the dining area, but also enabled their voices to come through. While the chain closing off the play area was of importance to the children; no adults seemed to bother and the hook remained broken during the entire spring, the glassed-in wall of the party room was a common concern for children, hostess, and parents. The hostesses implied that the visuality of the birthday parties was excellent advertising – the parties worked as live advertising signs for everybody in the dining area. The children acted as extras in this marketing play. Children often stood outside and looked in through the windows, and parents and children passing by often commented on what went on inside. The glassed-in walls also made it possible for the parents to control the happenings inside – both the hostess' and the children's actions. This possibility was not appreciated by the hostesses, who considered the parents as an interfering burden. The parents did however not use the glassed-in walls this way, at least not to check on the hostess. Instead they allowed them to keep track of the party proceedings, which allowed them to grab their cameras when it was time to open presents, or for some other memorable activity.

While the materiality of the premises afforded various actions for children, and parents, it was a definite hindrance for the execution of the theme parties, the hostesses told me. There were the other guests to consider, and the size of the children's corner, as well as the furnishing of the dining area, had definite limits as experience providers. To raise excitement it would have been necessary to do away with the restaurant building altogether. In many countries McDonald's birthday parties are in fact provided at other places than the restaurant. An example is the 'Jungle Book 2 Party' provided in India (!), where the children are invited to a guided safari in which they ride on elephant back through the jungle. The connection to McDonald's is the food (Happy Meals), party hats, presents and party bags. In a fascinating way this invented Disney story (based on a book by Rudyard Kipling), has become reality, and is performed with real elephants in the real jungle, and with a real Indian child as Mowgli (the role of birthday child) – consuming a Happy Meal.

It is therefore important not to conceive the restaurant as a fixed setting, or stage where the party is performed. Neither can it be regarded simply in terms of affordance; the restaurant is not only part of a global network, it is also 'on the move' although at a slower pace than for example the food, or customers. The same way that the party rituals are repetitions, the relational networks of actants performing chairs, tables, and kitchen machines are also 'repeating them' constantly, like 'reiterating refrains' (Brown and Capdevila, 1999). They are also, however, transforming; the dining area has changed a lot during the past few years; the ball rooms have been replaced by party corners, and the plastic balls were exchanged for climbing frames, the set furniture has been replaced by relaxed café-like furnishing, and most recently a whole new set of children's furniture has been introduced. The 'placeness' of the restaurant is thus an illusion. As Maria Brodin argues in the preceding chapter, referring to Bruno Latour (1997), there are no stable spaces, only more or less successful efforts to make space appear stable. The materiality of the restaurant is not essentially different from the materiality of the children, the staff, the burgers, and the dress-up clothes, or any other actor. The premises are also on the move. The same way as Brodin's furniture stores, the restaurant can be conceived as the consequence of the production and reproduction of relationships (Law, 2000), or as Carter and Michael (2002) put it, 'emerging out of a set of heterogeneous relationalities', in this case including food, furniture, technology, staff and customers.

Human and non-human actants

As a network the party consists of a vast amount of actors relationally generated by and generating the party, and thus the visible 'effects' or 'outcomes' of the party-net in action (Law, 1999). Each one of these actors might be studied as performed by distributed networks of human and non-human actants, the way for example the actor Fredrik and the other children in Barbro Johansson's chapter are. But keeping this in mind, for the time being they will be regarded as concentrated or even singular agents/agency (Michael, 2000). Not all of the once described below are actors with an own voice per se, such as the manual or the inscription of the theme party, but they all become (more or less) important agents in the party-net in action.

The birthday party manual: a circulating referent in the world-wide network of McDonald's restaurants listing the elements, and preferred trajectory of the standard McDonald's party: Happy Meal – games – parade to the kitchen – finding the treasure (Happy Meal boxes with the toy of the week, promotional coupons and leaflets) – the cutting of the cake – the gift-giving, including the special McDonald's gift to the birthday child. The props requested by the manual is Ronald McDonald table mats, party hats, napkins, balloons, the Happy Meal, gift boxes with promotional items, a McDonald birthday cake with candles, and the special Ronald gift to the birthday child. As an American invention from the sixties it reflects marketing strategies of the time of promoting customer loyalty by an abundance of McDonald's promotions. The very highlight of the manual is the parade to the kitchen to admire the soda fountain, and the ice-cream machine, to see the swinging of a hamburger, and to thank the staff for the food. The inscription of the child consumer is a fairly naive child, firmly fixed in a generational order, easy to please and sharing the amazement of Ray Kroc of the fantastic kitchen machines, and the efficiency of the hamburger production. It can be noted that the inscribed party is not just about consumption, but also about admiring the production process, and paying homage to the kitchen staff.

The new inscription of the theme parties as a play performed at the restaurant/theatre. On the homepage an ideal stage design was inscribed: 'Pale-faces, get down! The whole party corner is swarming with Red-Indian chiefs, warriors and squaws. Count in war dancing and Indian singing' (the Indian party). 'Lower the drawbridge and blow the trumpets! In the restaurant's hall of knights there will be nothing but heroic tales when beautiful princesses and brave knights from all over the kingdom gather to have a feast' (Princess and Knight). The homepage promises that the parties will be 'noisy, happy and at full speed', connoting a somewhat anarchistic childhood, and a competent child not easy to satisfy. It also promises to make the birthday child the center of attention; 'the king or queen of the day' inscribing an individualistic and competitive child. In addition 'fun stories', 'story time', and 'classical games' are promised repeating an inscription of a timid child put back into the generational order, and guided by adults in organized play and games. The crowding inscriptions were due to an effort to please the customer/parent by assembling all of the various symbolic objects and moments considered of interest for the parent. In the experience economy the customer is king. This inscription was, however, not yet translated to routines and objects at the restaurant; so far only to dress-up clothes contained in a chest in the staff dressing-room backstage, theme invitation cards, and place cards that could be printed from the homepage.

The party hostess: an important character in many ways. For the parents she was an absolutely essential ingredient of the party package, for many of them a main reason to have a party at McDonald's. It was also her job to translate the manual, and the theme party, into a performance at the restaurant. And she did so by using the skills and knowledge she had been taught at in-service training, and even more importantly, she used the tools and techniques that had been passed down from generation to generation of hostesses at the restaurant. The translating effort was to transform the parties into pedagogic events in accordance with daycare pedagogy, and to transform the hostess into a pedagogue. This way the party games had been replaced by 'free play', where the children play on their own terms without adult intervention, and preferably in an area made safe for them, which has been the preferred play mode in Swedish kindergartens since the 1970s' (Brembeck, 2004) and 'tiger painting', where the children's noses were painted black, and they were given black whiskers, and orange and black stripes on their cheeks and foreheads, also connoting a 'free' Nordic upbringing, and an anti-authoritarian daycare/child culture. The overarching objective of the hostess was to please the customers – children and parents – and to generate good value for the money.

The parents of the birthday party children: Fathers and mothers driving the children to the party and helping them with clothes and presents when arriving at the restaurant. The birthday child's mother often brought candy bags, or some special request, like lactose-free ice-cream, and she was the one paying for the party. She was often the only one staying during the whole party, but was happy to delegate the feeding, playing, and entertaining to the hostess. What mattered to her and to the other parents were the performance of the rituals of a 'proper' family party; the cake and candles, the singing of the birthday song, the opening of the presents, and she supervised that she got what she had paid for.

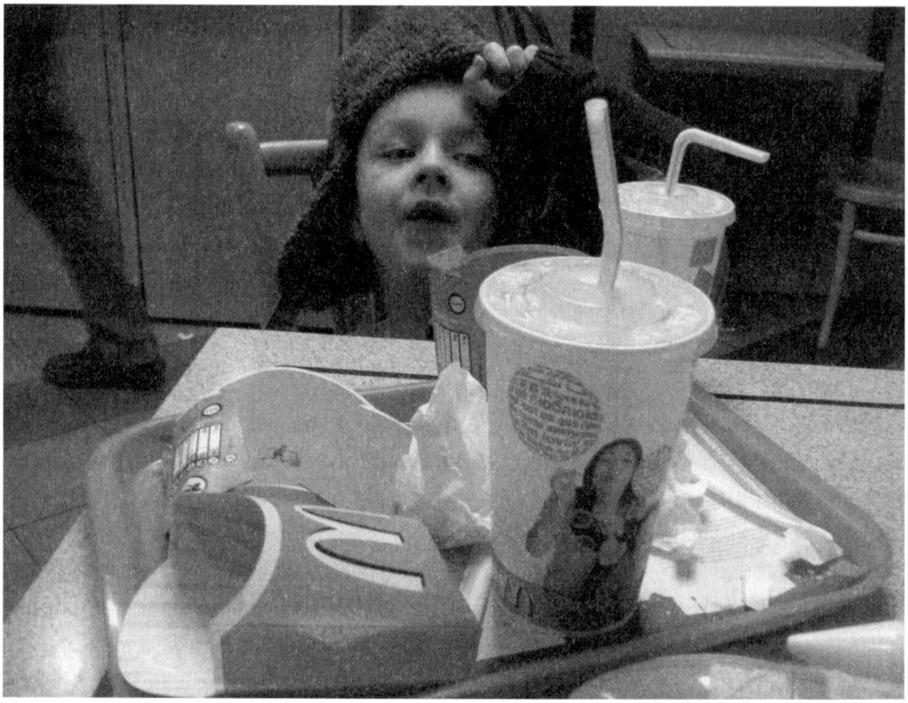

Johan at McDonalds's 2006. Photographer: Magnus Mörck.

The birthday party children: the leading actors and actresses, and the reason for throwing the party. They were the birthday child and approximately ten of her or his friends; boys and girls four to ten years of age. They brought their own presents, and the birthday child often brought a video to watch as well. The preferred trajectory, especially for the party guests, was to be able to be noisy and rowdy in the public space of the restaurant in ways they were not normally allowed to, to take possession of the dining area, to cross the border at the counter, get access to otherwise prohibited spaces, to be in control of the climbing frame, to shout out loud in the freezer – all things that were not normally allowed for children and that were not allowed for the rest of the children at the restaurant. On the whole they did their best to transform the party ritual into a game, and the restaurant into a playground.

In the black box is of course the very idea that there is such a thing as a birthday, moreover that this birthday shall be celebrated, and that this celebration requires certain rituals and props. Although the standard props for the children's birthday party in Anglo-American bourgeois family rituals were set already in the middle of the 19th century: sweets, cake and candles, presents and cards (Pleck, 2000), it is obvious that the black box is starting to leak in regard to these issues. This gives room for questioning, and innovations as well as anxiety. Should the presents be expensive or cheap? Does the party have to be at home or can it be executed in a public space? Should it be an ice gateau or a baked cake? Should there be fruit or sweets in the candy bags, or no candy bags at all? It is this leakage that all the actors take advantage of in the translation of the party ritual and props in accordance with their own ideas and ambitions.

The monstrous party

Taking the manual and its set party order as the starting point, it is easy to see that both children and hostesses acted as 'parasites' (Serre, 1982) disturbing, yet some times contributing to the prescribed party order. The children were distracted by children outside of the party room, and started to make faces through the window instead of giving attention to what went on inside. They did not consume the hamburgers, they did not line up properly for the parade to the kitchen. The hostesses did not support admiration for kitchen equipment, and I only once saw a hamburger getting swung, and then it was done in quite a humorous manner. The theme parties transformed the parade to the kitchen into a treasure hunt ending by the freezer, where the treasure – Happy Meal boxes – was hidden. The children liked the toy in the gift box, but did not care much for the promotional coupons, leaflets, and the special McDonald's gift to the birthday child which had a long time ago been replaced with pencils and erasers. The hostess willingly administered candy bags from the birthday child's mother, and made the giving of the presents from the party guests one of the most outstanding rituals of the party.

The children were also disturbing the hostess' pedagogic inventions. Although most of them agreed to get their faces painted, the tiger painting promoted by the hostesses was not so popular. The girls preferred to be painted like princesses, cats or rabbits, and some of them wanted only little red hearts discretely put on their arms like small tattoos. For the boys Spiderman was the preferred request this spring, probably because of the release of the Spiderman film around Christmas. Several children, however, did not really know what to do about the face painting. One little boy wanted to be painted like Tarzan (who does not have a face painting, nor does he wear a mask in the series), and after some embarrassment he realizes this, and wants to be Spiderman like the rest of the boys. Approaching Easter some of the children wanted to be painted like Easter witches, a tradition which is part of the Swedish Easter celebration, and does not belong to the party ritual. And then of course, there were the ones who did not want to be painted at all.

In performing the party, the uniformity of the party ritual according to the manual, turned to several competing trajectories, making the party a special kind of ordering, possible to be framed differently by the different actors, involving diverse highlights, sacrifices, and gains. The children have to submit in many ways to the orders of the adults: march in line, subject to face painting, and public inspection through the windows of the party room, but they also gain competence in mastering public spaces as if they were almost like at home. In comparison with the prescribed theme parties on the homepage, there were no traditional party games conducted, and no stories read. The individualistic offers to be 'at the center' and to be 'king and queen for a day' were downplayed. A bystander could hardly distinguish the birthday child from the rest of the children, at least not until the opening of the presents. Instead pedagogic elements like free play and face painting, a noisy atmosphere, and an equal relation between the children and the young hostess was the rule. The McDonald's birthday party proved to be a monster.

Performing little monsters

As the party-net starts acting, the child constantly bumps into actants, belonging to other networks providing it with (new, transformed) agency, subjectivity, intentionality, and morality, eventually generating the 'string figure' (Martin, 1997) of the becoming birthday child, condensed but always also dispersed (on children as becomings, see the chapter by Johansson). We will now focus a few of these momentary networks specifically to look at consuming birthday party personas – little monsters – being performed, starting with the joyful child-commander of the climbing frame, the concerned negligent parent and the hostess-pedagogue.

Repetitions from daycare

It is obvious that the children were well accustomed as consumers of public services like daycare, and school, and they brought knowledge and techniques from these institutions to the party. The power games played in the climbing frame seemed to be a repetition of innumerable similar acts at the yard of the daycare, school, or home, as the way to trustingly come running to the hostess to get help when offended. Not only were the hostesses performing techniques from child care pedagogy, but also the children. They had already learnt the lesson that possessing materiality, like the climbing frame gives power. The existence of a climbing frame enabled and suggested repetitions of such power play, but not for all children: only some grasped the possibility to be in command of the other children, most of them were too timid, shy or accustomed with a more subordinate position. Instead the regular power balance between the children seemed to re-establish. So, the child persona as commander of the climbing frame, was performed by a network consisting of the child-centered pedagogy, (the idea of as well as subjectivity of) the competent child, the importance of free play, the concept of the customer as king, and the narrowness of the party room. It also contributed to the negligence of the adults, making the power play of the children somewhat of a hidden agenda not noted by parents or staff.

This repetition of consumer attitudes from the public service field not only concerned the children, but also their parents. They relied on the fact that the children were used to be taken care of by unknown persons, like substitutes at school, and they relied on that they were able to handle the situation without anxiety. They were also grateful for the pedagogic competence of the hostess to guide the children through the party routines. Some of the hostesses even suggested that the children behaved better when guided by an unknown person. This service was in fact what mattered most to them. The children generally considered the hostess as nice, while the parents complimented her good hands with the children. It is obvious that the pedagogic additions to the party were not only whims on the side of the hostesses, trying to give their work more of a professional status, but generated in a network including the parents, the children, public discourses of child pedagogy, the other guests at the restaurant, and also the furnishing of the children's corner like the climbing frame.

Other consuming birthday personas were performed that were not as much repetitions from daycare, but had more to do with the restaurant as a public commercial space: what I would like to call non-commitment/commitment switching, and a readiness to be consumed by others. We will study this by framing a few moments of the party-net in action, starting with the performance of non-commitment.

Performing non-commitment

First let's wind our story back to the children running out of the party room, leaving their hamburgers half-eaten, and their fries all over the table, and the hostess tidying up the greasy left-overs. The consumer agency performed is obviously one of non-commitment sanctioned by the adults. How can the children show such disrespect to the 'All-American hamburger', and how can they get away with it? A birthday party is a special event, and it includes the consumption of food, not just the cake and sweets, but also some more filling food considered tasty and festive by the party guests, like the fillet of pork and the potatoes au gratin at a wedding dinner (Salomonsson, 2006). One of the scary things about having a party at home for the parents/mothers was not to be able to serve the children something they really liked, and – even more scary – that they would refuse the food, so that she would not be able to fulfill the duty of feeding them. That guests leave a party hungry is a nightmare for any hostess, pointing to the significance of the food to transform the party into a special event. The anxiety of not being able to make the children content is one of the reasons why the party was held at McDonald's. It was a safe card; the mother knew that they liked hamburgers and fries, and that the obligation to feed them would be achieved.

For the children, however, hamburgers were nothing special. Maybe they were thirty years ago, when McDonald's was new, and held an infinite aura of newness, and exiting Americanism for many Swedes. But for today's children hamburgers, and Coca-Cola are very mundane artifacts, and the Happy Meal hold no ritual or sacred features what so ever for them (Brembeck, 2005). So this sacred artifact of the company was not at all able to transform the meal into a festive dinner. The children longed for the enjoyment of the climbing frame, and the privileges of being kings and queens of the play area for a while. The hostess knew about this, and her ambition of giving the customer (child, parent) what they wanted – an experience out of the ordinary/good value for money – in her mind translated into suitable pedagogical activities, like face painting and free play: all of this made the meal nothing more than something that just had to be carried through.

There were, in fact, some ritual components in taking the children's orders at the table, which was nothing ordinary at McDonald's. But for the children this was mundane as they were accustomed to the way their parents used to go about doing it when they visited the restaurant with their families. They showed ease and competence in the situation, obviously knowing the Happy Meal selections already at four years of age (the youngest age of a child attending a party). When the hostess returned, she was carrying the burgers and fries stacked more or less in a mess on the tray, and they were then shoved to the children around the table. Often some child sitting close to the hostess would help her out by standing on a chair, and more or less throwing the orders to the children around the table. The meals ended up being disordered, and no measure was taken to set the table properly. This was due to the size of the birthday room with the table and chairs almost completely filling the room, leaving no space for the hostess to walk around, and hardly for the children, making them walk on the chairs, and take short-cuts over as well as under the table.

In every way the burgers were shown disrespect. During the meal a video film was watched, and the attention and comments of the children were directed towards it. They were picking at their burger and fries without even looking at them, making them even more insignificant. All of the children were however eating some of their meals, though several only ate the fries, and they were thus meeting the wish of the parent/mother of feeding the children. To sum up; the non-committing child persona was performed by a network consisting of the ordinariness of the burger for the children, and the hostess' knowledge of this, as well as her ambitions to give the children what they wanted (play), and also of including value-for-money pedagogic activities (free play and face painting; in fact the face painting was no longer included in the standard party, and had to be paid extra for, but at this restaurant the hostesses continued to carry it out without charging any extra, because they wanted the parents to have good value for money), more over the narrowness of the party room, and the disordered serving of the meal. Another example of the performance of non-commitment to artifacts of high importance to McDonald's, was the way the children totally ignored the discount coupons and promotional leaflets they found in the Happy Meal box/treasure in the freezer. As small pieces of paper covered with letters and figures, they had little to say to the children, or maybe they just resembled the direct advertisement their parents were throwing away at home. Not even the Happy Meal toys were always appreciated by all children, and there were generally one or two of them left on the floor, or discarded at some table, when the children left the restaurant.

This attitude of non-commitment might be interpreted as performed by spoilt children and the compliant staff and 'curling parents' sweeping the floor and all troubles away for their fickle children (Hougaard, 2004). From a network perspective it instead emerges as a pivotal technique for handling everyday life in a society overflowing with objects. What might look as negligence turns out to be a competence of letting go, passing by and/or not bothering which are necessary for survival in consumer culture. Just as necessary is the competence of switching back to commitment, and when and how to do this.

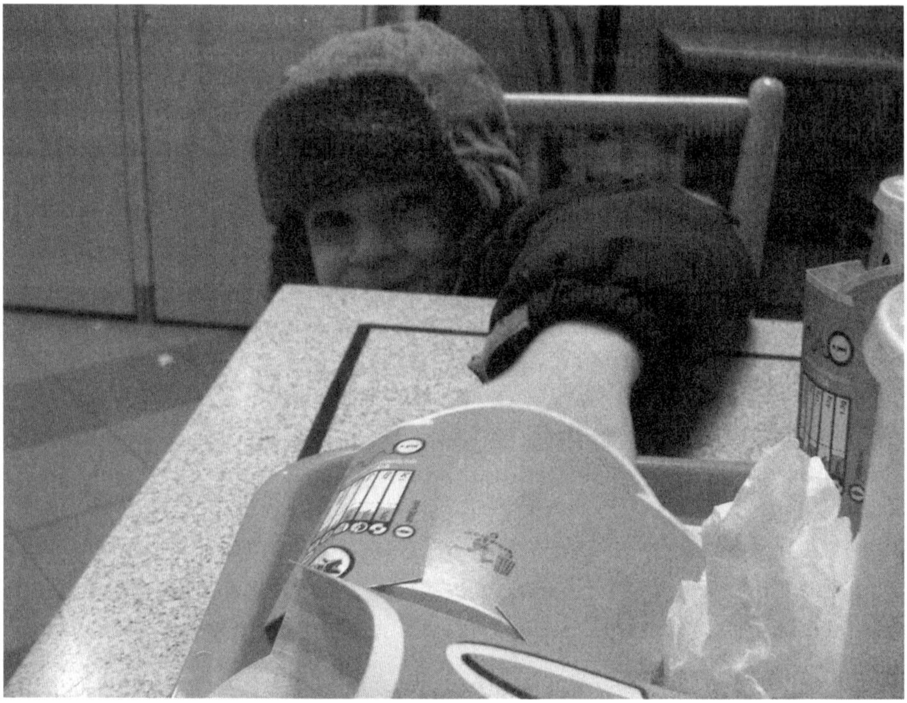

Johan at McDonalds's 2006. Photographer: Magnus Mörck.

Switching to commitment

Now let's turn to another type of scenery. Once again the children are assembled around the table in the party room, but with quite another objective in mind. It is at the end of the party, and it is time for the birthday child to open the presents. They have been piled above the TV in the party room during the entire party, where everybody can see them, making the TV set somewhat of an altar of the party room. This is where all eyes have been fixated during video watching. The parents crowd in the doorway with their cameras and camcorders to document this special moment. The hostess turns towards the presents, and the children get very quiet and attentive watching her. She reaches for one present at a time from above the TV set, and hands it over to the birthday child, who quickly opens it. The hostess then holds it high up for all the children to see, and it is admired and commented. 'Who brought this present?' she asks, and the giver reports him/herself. Sometimes the birthday child comes forward to say thank you, or even hug the giver, who is momentarily given almost more attention than the birthday child. The act of reaching, handing over, opening, admiring, holding high, and recognizing the giver is repeated over and over again, until all presents are delivered.

The last present is the special McDonald's gift. At the restaurant it consists of pencils, erasers, bookmarks and the like, instead of the standard Ronald McDonald's mug, plate, and cutlery. The children had grown tired of the Ronald porcelain according to the hostesses. Many of them had been to McDonald's parties before, and had already a set at home. Something extra seems to be needed, and one of the hostesses used to buy cheap little things – that she considered were more attractive for the children – on her own. The special McDonalds's gift is thus quite humble in regard to the presents from the friends, and can in no way compete with them in economic value or exclusiveness. It is not given much attention, but is recognized, and all the birthday children get to bring one home. Now the party ends, and the hostess puts the presents in one bag and the wrapping paper in another. What is really happening, and how come the hostess willingly allows the private gifts from the children to be included in the party, translating the giving away of them into a central ritual of the party?

It is very important for the parents that this moment gets more attention than anything else at the party (besides the cutting of the cake, and the singing of the birthday song). It is of course also essential for the children, and for the parents of the other children. Without presents there is no birthday. Referring to rites of passages, it seems as if the transformation from one age to another can only be performed by the help of the ritual sacrifice of presents from the friends. For a moment the child is generated as almost 'divine', entering a constructed liminality necessary for the passage. McDonald's presents (Happy Meal boxes and the special gift to the birthday child) are not enough. Without this gift-giving ritual the birthday party would simply not be 'real'. Moreover the parent would not be interested in paying for the party, if the guests were not allowed to bring their own presents.

The power of the gift is the way it creates relational ties between the giver and receiver; if you give me something, I have to give back if I want to stay your friend. In consumer culture, this means giving a gift of equal value (Miller, 1999). In the process of admiring the gifts, and naming the giver, some gifts were appreciated more, and given more attention by the children, and this had not only to do with the size, price or exclusivity of the gift. Relational ties, friendships, status hierarchies as well as agreement with what was hot stuff in child culture at the moment played a great part. Pedagogic gifts like books, chosen by some ambitious parent, were generally not given as much attention as for example dolls, or action figures, although the hostesses tried to support the giver. Reciprocity mattered most in groups of immigrant children. At many of these parties the gifts were really outstanding, and expensive, like Wedding Barbies with complete wardrobes. At one such party I could see how the little birthday child tried hard to memorize all the givers. When I asked her afterwards which present she liked the most, she enumerated all the givers with their presents, starting with the giver. To remember the connection between the person and the present was obviously more important than evaluating which presents were the most precious to her.

The consumer subjectivity being performed is obviously one of commitment, a committing persona is generated. The momentum of exchanging gifts with friends appears important, something to care about, where a switch from non-commitment to commitment is enabled. The gifts are singularized, and personalized in an almost ritual way. They are covered in wrapping paper, cutting the link to the market, when the hostess hands them over, and this paper is removed in front of the other children, and the content is revealed. The present is held high above the hostess' head like a sacred grail, and is then personified by naming the giver. The telling of the name and the way the giver is put forward are important as they provide a way of linking the present with a known person with a name. It becomes the present from Kalle or Lisa, even Kalle's or Lisa's present, obscuring whose present it really is; the giver's or the receiver's, maybe it for a moment belongs to both of them, forming a child-present-child unity, a true commercial-culture monster.

Now it becomes clear that no present from McDonald's could be given recognition at this moment. A Ronald plate (unwrapped) remains an anonymous plate from an anonymous giver, and is not able to pass the test of commitment, but remains something not worth engaging in. This is probably what the hostess in charge sensed when she bought little things herself, wrapping them in nice paper like the rest of the gifts. However she still declared it as a gift from McDonald's, not from her personally. It was never recognized as an important object, but was still brought home, and not left on the table like the promotional items. Had she presented the present as a gift from herself (personifying it), which it was, it probably would have received more attention. Had she said that she was giving it just because she wanted to make friends with the child (creating relational ties), which would not have been completely untrue, it would probably have received even more.

A mode of being consumed

The theme parties 'Princess and Knight' and 'Indians' were promoting the dining area as a stage, and the children as play-actors, a concept that should not to be mistaken for the ANT concept actor, although Bruno Latour welcomes some confusion. It is not by accident, he argues, that the word actor comes from the stage: 'play-acting puts us immediately into a thick imbroglio where the question of who is carrying out the action has become unfathomable.' (Latour, 2005:46). This is also certainly true of the play-acting at the party. Not only should the 'theme' transform the party into an event, it should transform the whole restaurant into an 'exciting place where fun things happen, not only a place where you quickly eat your hamburger and then leave', as one of the hostesses told me. A stop at the restaurant should be an experience for everybody, a display event for customers, too. The glassed-in party room and the dress-up clothes back stage contributed to this image. The stage design was provided on the homepage in terms of war dancing, Indian singing and princesses and knights gathering to have a feast.

At the restaurant the themed birthday parties were however not coming along so well. There were too many obstacles for the perfect experience to happen. First of all it was too expensive. An extra charge was requested for the dress-up clothes so many parents passed on that option. Neither were the clothes very effective in contributing to the experience. They were of bad quality and made of a stretch fabric, which did not at all give the body the posture and stability that would have been needed in order to create the right feeling (see e.g. Mathiesen Hjemdahl, 2003). The princess dresses were shapeless and only came in one size. The rubber band around the waist was sagging which made the skirt hems too long and caused at least the smallest of the princesses to stumble along in not a very princess-like manner. The limp knight hoods which hung over the boys' eyes and disturbed their play were soon thrown to the floor. There were no heroic tales and no Indian singing. The children had few references to how to behave as knights or Indians, and the hostesses had no training in drama. The clothes and dramaturgy would need to be of better quality in order for the themed parties to work. The most theatrical moment was in fact the face painting, but as we have already seen, many children were subverting this by asking for a little 'tattoo' on their arms instead, which they discretely hid underneath their sleeves, and thereby effectively destroying the theatrical concept.

The belief that play-acting as princesses and knights at a theme party is a way to amuse children and give them a high-quality experience, stems from an inscription of the child in experience economy as a stage actor – that play-acting for others comes naturally and that this is what children most of all want and aspire to. Similar ideas such as 'opening up, and acting out your inner dreams and passions in front of an audience allowing you to really come alive – your 15 minutes of fame, – can also be conceived as the most desirable experience for children as well as adults today (Bauman, 2002). The children, however, were not very comfortable in the role. Initially some were looking worriedly for their parents (who were hiding among the green plants of the restaurant not to be seen by the children – their idea was that the party should relieve them of responsibility, and they trusted the children's competence to handle the situation, and relied on the hostess). Entering the show case of the party room caused a considerable amount of anxiety.

The idea of the child as an aspiring play-actor is dependant on the conception of the child as a person with innate desires, and a personality residing in the child's body wanting to play games. However the argument in this chapter is that the child, agency, subjectivity, desires and competences are generated in networks, that is, an acting persona is the result of or effect of a network in action. In the real-life performance of the parties, the children did not know what was expected of them, and they felt shy and awkward in the situation, the clothes did not work, the hostesses were no dramaturges, the restaurant guests had not chosen to go to McDonald's to become spectators; on the whole the themed parties had not been successful in generating play-acting personas.

In the inscription of the theme parties there is also an idea that consuming events by watching them is an invigorating, as well as a relaxing experience that does not demand anything except attention. 'Lean back and enjoy your child's big day', as the homepage enticed. The concept of children amusing adults also reflects former times. In the Middle Ages small children were regarded as 'funny little monkeys' performing tricks amusing adults (Ariès, 1962), not to mention the bourgeois child performing tableaux for their parents' guests one or two hundred years ago (Pleck, 2000). Most parents, however, desperately needed some time off for their own chores, and had no interest in watching the party. Some of them, like the birthday children's mothers, did want a relaxing time; instead they wanted to be relieved of the responsibilities of getting involved in the party. This is why they kept out of the children's sight; they knew that if their child would have caught sight of them, they would immediately be transformed from anonymous guests into responsible parents. So the parents did not feel comfortable with the role as spectators of their children's McDonald's party. The party net was not able to transform them into an audience. The only moment they showed interest in the party was when it was time for the cutting of the cake, the birthday song, and the presents. Then they all appeared not, however, as an anonymous audience, but as parents to their children taking part in the celebration of the big day of the birthday child.

So the children never became play-actors. But apart from some initial anxiety when entering the party room/show case, they did not seem to care much that others were watching, and they were fairly unmoved of what went on outside of the party room. Momentarily they had lots of visual contact with parents, or other children on the other side of the windows, which was interpreted by the hostesses as a lack of concentration. In these cases the windows involved problems. The hostesses had in fact considered providing curtains for the windows to reduce the risk of disturbances, but also to make the party room cozier, and more of a secret place for the children. But this idea did not last long, something that is quite understandable considering the fact that the prime function of the party room is to act as a show case. It is also noticeable that when the children spotted me and my camera, several of them gave an almost reflexive smile, even posing – while others were disinterested, and a few even a bit irritated, and in those cases I of course quickly turned the camera away. They performed the party – not as play-actors, but simply as children at a birthday party – with ease, apparently little bothered by the other people watching them. They were even taking advantage of the privileges the visuality gave them in respect to other children; making faces at by-passers while protected by the party setting and the thick glass walls. What were being performed were not child play-actors, but a readiness to be visually consumed by others. For some, this might in fact be the first steps in the transformation into the posing child persona performing in TV shows as artists, adventurers, or gamblers.

The making of McChildhood

To perform this switch between non-commitment and commitment, holding and letting go, and this special competence in managing over-abundance, no split between public and private is needed. It all happens at the co-joint time space of the restaurant, hybridizing family values/home and commercialism/public, signified by the bringing of private presents, bought in shops, and wrapped in expensive wrapping paper to celebrate this private ritual in the public place of the restaurant. Commercial culture settings produce commercial culture subjectivities and competencies. In this melange of actors, trajectories, transformations, inscriptions and affordances, a McDonald's/Swedish childhood is performed at once condensed and distributed. Swedish ideas on childrearing, Disney toys, the tiredness of the parents, the power fights, the media knowledge of the children, and the shapelessness of the dresses all contributed in generating the competences, identities and preferences which constitute the McChild and the McChildhood; anti-authoritarian and child-centered, yet supervised, regulated and communal.

III

Precious Monsters

Wedding in a Box – Foldings of Time and Space

Eva KNUTS

A wedding keepsake box? The first time I came across one of them I was amused, intrigued and puzzled and I wondered what the box would contain and why. Since then I have finished my thesis about weddings [1] and I have read about the boxes on the Internet, and now finally made one. [2] Some of the items in the box were lent to me by one of my transformants [3] and others I had collected during my time in the wedding field – things that are recommended in ads and in wedding magazines to be kept in the box. I have the box, a lot of stuff to put into it but I don't have the memories that should be connected to the box.

It is obvious that the box in front of me – and the boxes sold on the Internet – has something to do with weddings. There is a certain aesthetic that gives it away. It is decorated with white satin, lace and pearls. On the lid there is a space for attaching a photo (of the happy couple) or a nametag e.g. it could be the names and the date of the wedding. The box is anonymous but can be personalized by this device. The box's external dimensions are 35 cm (13.78 in.) long, 30 cm (11.81 in.) wide and 10 cm (3.94 in.) high – not very big in other words. The box including its contents weighs a little bit more than 1 kg. It is heavier in one corner and I know it's because there is a glass bottle with perfume there and a cake topping in the form of a wedding couple.

At the bottom of the box there is a scrapbook with a white cover which matches the box. I will look into it later on in this chapter. Another album contains photos in black and white. It looks very professional.

---

1 My thesis is written in Swedish and has the title:*Något gammalt, något nytt – skapandet av bröllopsföreställningar.* (Something old, something new – the creation of wedding performances) (Knuts, 2006).

2 I made the box the same size as one I found on the Internet. I used fabric that was left over from a wedding dress I made once upon a time when I worked as a dress maker. I very carefully studied what the boxes on Internet look like. In my case this box will be, by the time I have finished this chapter and returned the memorabilia I have borrowed, used to store things in connection to my thesis and disputation, a kind of memory box with wedding items but without a wedding!

3 I stopped calling the people I met and interviewed informants, which is the common word for Swedish ethnologists to use, according to Latour's book *Reassembling the Social* .(Latour, 2005). 'There is no in-formation, only trans-formation' (ibid: 149), there can be no *in*formants, only *trans*formants.

In a folder there is an invitation card, program for the ceremony, menu and thank you cards. They all match each other with gold, brown and white covers and with the same typeface. When I open the thank you card, I look at the faces of the couple who were kind enough to lend me some of their memorabilia.

A small pillow, made out of white satin with lace on the edges and strings in the middle, reminds us of the rings. The rings were tied to this pillow during the ceremony until they were released and put on the couple's fingers. The rings themselves are not, of course, in the box. The couple wears them on their fingers as a daily reminder. There are two other items made out of fabric: a pair of white gloves and a small handbag with pearls attached to it.

A CD with a picture of the couple and their names and the date is also found in the box. I put the CD into my player. It begins with Mendelssohn's wedding march! Then there are a lot of the couple's favorite songs. I know they played this CD at the wedding. There are also two other CDs: one containing photos, hundreds of them in digital form, and the other a digital film from the wedding.

In a small box inside the box there are flowers that look remarkably fresh. I will tell you why later on. I find a guest book where the couple is greeted by their loved ones. In an envelope there are tickets which tell me where they went on their honeymoon. There are also photos from the trip in the envelope. I guess that they are going to put them in an album but haven't had the time, yet.

The box and what it contains will be the main character in this chapter. I will deal with it from several perspectives: the materiality in the box, memory and time, preservation techniques and how a multiplicity in the end of an organizing process can become black – or in this case – 'white boxed'.

Precious matter…

'My precious', said Gollum about the golden ring that gave the owner extended life time (Tolkien, 1954). Like Gollum, I guess, we all want to extend experiences we enjoy, it can be life or it can be a wedding. We value things that might help us achieve that and they become precious to us.

A wedding keepsake box can be a small, precious monster.[4] The value is not economical, even though these boxes can cost around $ 50; the value

[4] 'Wedding keepsake boxes' are not the only precious monsters; there are boxes to store memories of pets, sacraments, childhood and baptism e.g. (www.findgift.com/Categories/Keepsake/Memory-Boxes).

comes from the investment in the time and effort that are put into it and the things it will contain. The value lies in what it *becomes* not what it *is* when someone purchases it. Even though the box, and most of its content, is mass-produced items, it becomes appreciated by the married couple through its ability to keep memories alive when personalized items are put into it. The box will, ultimately, bare the essence of a couple's wedding. It will contain specially selected items that will sum up this extraordinary day, and that is when it gets its value.

On the Internet 'wedding keepsake boxes' are sold with accompanying texts focusing on the idea that materiality has the power to keep wedding memories alive.

> 'All the joy, fun, emotions and special moments of weddings stays forever in the hearts of brides and grooms with help of keepsakes. The power of photograph, a corner of lace, a honeymoon ticket, or a scribbled note written by your grandmother transcends mere memory and brings you back to the moment, without a care for the passage of time' (www.Familyjewelsarchivals.com 2005 – 08 – 15).

This phenomena to collect, conserve, protect is a way of thinking that time can be stopped, at least in a small, local place. Closed in a box you can keep your wedding unaffected by time and by reopening the box you can bring back the wedding exactly as it was, not changed at all. Perhaps even a little bit better.

Before I proceed with the discussion about the box I want to make a short notice on memory and changed attitudes toward memories and how various actors connect memories to materiality.

Memorabilia at the market

There is a market for memories. Memories and feelings are exploited to sell both experiences and commodities. Memories are said, in ads, to be irreplaceable, as if they were something stable – being – and not in a continuum – becoming – in a never-ending open-ended process. Some of the keywords in the ads connected to keepsake boxes are: 'intact', 'keep', 'forever' and 'bring back'. These words are intermixed with sometimes paradox descriptions of how memories work. Memories are said to be both unforgettable and at the same time in need of memorabilia. This suggests an interesting way of locating memories not only as stored in human brains, but as something that needs input of a different kind. In ads for keepsake boxes the idea that memories can

A wedding keepsake box. The external dimensions are 35 cm (13.78 in) long, 30 cm (11.81 in.) wide and 10 cm (3.94 in.) high. Inside it is covered with brown satin and outside with white silk and it has pearls and ribbons as a decoration on the lid. Some of the things seen here are 'Thank-you-card', tiara, a small handbag with pearls which matched the tiara and the jewelry worn at the wedding. We see a ring pillow and a glimpse of a guest-book in which near and dear have written greetings during the wedding reception. Photographer: Eva Knuts

get lost, distorted or misplaced gives the argument to buy and fill them. Memories are not something that just exist and thrive but they also need to be worked on to maintain alive. But on the other hand they are seen in a straight timeline where memories can pile up and accumulate over time, as if they would never change.

This view of memories, as in need of constant input, is easy to associate with ideas of human and non-human actors constantly connecting in networks. As Pepperell argues: 'Human thoughts are not a hermetic, linier system. Since we know that the mind, body and environment cannot be separated, we cannot rule out the impact of any environmental stimuli on the process of thoughts, no matter how minute it might seem' (Pepperell, 2003:186). Both human and non-human actors constantly connect with each other. There is no dichotomy between human and non-humans, between material things and social influences, only differences in the tempo of changeability.

When I first came across a wedding keepsake box, some years ago, I hadn't seen any in Sweden before, only on Internet. My parents got married in the 60's and they didn't even have a shoe box to collect wedding items in. They did save things, but they didn't arrange them in any certain way and they didn't organize their wedding with the idea of creating memories. They were more concerned with collecting things for the home that they were about to create together. There are just a few remembrances of their wedding: a champagne cork, photos and my mother's wedding ring.

My transformants, who have married during the past five years, have kept many more things from their weddings than my parents' generation did. They collected items all through the wedding preparation, even if not all of them had bought a special box to store it in. The boxes are now starting to be mentioned in wedding magazines and in chat-rooms on the Internet in Sweden. I'm convinced that keepsake boxes will conquer the Swedish market. There are many actors working for them. When I Google the word 'memorabilia' a lot of companies that sell scrapbooks, keepsake boxes and books about how to 'craft heritage' and even guides on how to 'create heritage' are shown. Some of the companies that sell scrapbooks, a growing hobby in Sweden, also sell memory boxes. The inspiration from one form of crafting heritage leaks into another and keepsake boxes get more attention than before.

What is new today is that there is a market for memories: an industry that draws heavily on people's fear to forget. Memories have become a commercially negotiable commodity. Advertisements and marketing stress that time is something that has to be fought. Memories are precious; ads argue it is an investment to preserve an expensive wedding.

Wedding keepsake box – Deluxe size

'A truly unique way to preserve all the memories of your special day!' (www.personalizationmall.com). This truly unique deluxe box is a little bit bigger than the average one (52 x 35 x10 cm) and the customer can personalize it by adding 'first names and wedding date, stamped permanently on the lid in silver foil' (ibid) by entering the names (up to 20 characters) and the date on the company's webpage. Unfortunately no 'foreign' letters, like the Swedish ones, can be used. People with names like Åsa, Örjan or Håkan can't get a personalized box. Or perhaps you choose the 'Wedding Days Luxe Scrapbook & Keepsake Box Gift Set'? 'Our Scrapbook & matching Keepsake Box is the perfect gift and will hold infinitive memories and keepsake for a lifetime' (www.aimeej.com). In addition, the gift set can be personalized by adding names.

Finding the right present can be difficult. Some of these boxes, like the one above, are sold as gifts; of course the couple can buy them for themselves as well. But some of my transformants received scrapbooks or other memory sakes as presents. The mother/mother-in-law or friends started the collection and the couple is supposed to continue filling the album or memory box. When a keepsake box has made it in to a couple's wedding (at this early stage it doesn't have to be physically present, the idea is enough) it starts to act as a gravity center. Some of the non-human actors, like a keepsake box, involved in the making of a wedding invite others into the wedding network. 'Each artifact has a script, its potential to take hold of passersby and force them to play role in its story' (Latour, 1999:177). The box takes hold of passersby and may even purchase items for the wedding!

The keepsake box can be seen as a cluster that starts to attract other non-humans and humans. In making wedding plans, there are often intentions which can be seen as purely human. When a couple sketches out a wedding they often have an idea of the result. Other human beings are given responsibilities along the way to the altar and so is materiality, consequently even if the idea of a wedding's composition seems to come from human actors this gets blurry as materiality will get tasks along the way. This is a perspective I will get back to: stabilization through materiality, technologies and chemical preparation.

An empty box does not fulfill its purpose. Boxes are seldom bought just to be a box but to store things in. A box in white satin with your name on the lid is hard to ignore. An empty box can be a way to show: we don't have any nice wedding memories. What? No nice things to remind us of the 'most memorable occasions of one's lifetime' (www.indianchild.com/wedding). The box will be filled! But it is not determined, yet, what will end up in the box. There are still a lot of negotiations to be made before the box will contain the ultimate essence of a couple's wedding. But it has already started to affect the outcome. The box is empty and craves attention and things to be filled with.

A wedding keepsake box plans a wedding

'Still I'm an empty space. I look real nice which is more than I can say about that other box. Why are they just putting things into that? But my time will come, I'm sure.'

All my transformants, including the ones who had lavish weddings and the ones who had smaller weddings, had a temporary 'box' (it could also be a drawer or some other place) where they kept everything that had to do with the preparation of the wedding. The first idea of a guest list, recipes for inspiration, wedding magazines with post-it notes attached to pictures of dresses, rings or other items they had not yet decided on, 'to-do lists', budgets, receipts, contracts, color samples, samples of invitation cards and so on. The wedding preparation leaves a lot of material traces. Some of these traces will be thrown away, as it is just working material. At this point, it is still too early to say what will end up in the adorned box. One piece of advice that keeps coming back is: 'As soon as there is a hint of a wedding, set up a file to collect pictures and other memorabilia. Because you are going to be so overwhelmed with wedding preparation, don't take the time to evaluate every saved item. /.../ Just collect everything that's come along – you'll be able to sort the items once the wedding day is over' (*www.idsweddings.com*).

From a 'to-do list' [5] one can find some stages in the wedding preparation that should be documented:

- Engagement and wedding announcements from the newspaper.
- The complete wedding invitation, as well as invitations to the engagement party, bridal showers, and rehearsal dinner.

[5] Even if this list is recommended for scrapbooking the ideas to collect memories are much the same as to filling a keepsake box. Scrapbooks are also often a part of the contents of a box.

- Mementos from bridal showers, bridesmaids luncheon, or other pre-wedding get-togethers.
- Look up the couple's honeymoon destination on the Internet, and print some enticing images of the honeymoon destination.
- Wedding ceremony and reception mementos, including favors, imprinted napkins, ceremony programs, and table decorations.
- Pictures! Keep a camera handy to snap photos of the happy couple in the months leading up to the wedding, and of course, make sure to get lots of snapshots on the wedding day!' (*http://www.lexmark.com/uncomplicate/sequentialem/home/0,7070,239544855_482420577_0_en,00.html* (2006–12–06)).

A wedding is an event that takes place during one day. But the preparation, organization and structuring can go on for a long time, both before and after the wedding. The time, money and energy that people, in today's Swedish society, spend on their weddings are increasing, so is the number of people getting married. Today it is normal to plan a wedding for a year or more. 'Like most other culturally significant performances, weddings require elaborate preparations, with magazines commonly providing a timetable for things that should be done as much as two years before the actual wedding' (Anderson, 2000:50). And during the planning of a wedding the couple (and friends and relatives) are encouraged to save everything that has to do with the wedding! At this point, the box has still not decided what to keep but it cheers on all kind of activities – like bridal showers (unknown in Sweden, but we have hen parties .(Knuts, 2007)), honeymoons, engagement parties, newspaper announcements – that can fill its empty space. However the activities can't be stored, they have to be anchored with some kind of materiality.

Before I deal with the materiality in the box I want take a step back in the wedding preparation, and briefly discuss different trajectories in the wedding field which will affect the content of the box, or is it the other way around?

Peak performance

The peak of a wedding is during one day, even if weddings tend to become a weekend affair. However the preparation can go on for a long time, as I have stated earlier. From the beginning a wedding can be relatively open and loosely knitted. 'Brain-storming' in the beginning can take all kinds of directions. Few things are decided even if some circumstances, like budget, frame the fantasies. But as soon as some connections are translated through materiality, technologies or/and utterance they start to form clusters and the motion slows down. 'Networks or assemblages of extensions expand and incorporate more and more elements. The bigger the assemblages, the slower it can change or be changed' (Lee, 2001:137). As soon as clusters are formed they start to act as gravitation centers, they tie some actors to them and exclude others.

'We use to ask about where the wedding will take place. If it will be a small ceremony in a garden you have to choose a different dress than if it is a lavish church wedding. So of course the basic condition plays a part in choosing the dress', says a wedding shopkeeper I have interviewed. This quote is an example of how some decisions, in this case the type of ceremony, bring certain materiality into the network, or it might as well be the other way around: a dress chooses the ceremony venue. The dress will, in the next step, pull accessories that go with it into the wedding. The outcome is not as open-ended as it was during the first 'brain-storming' meeting.

There are 'maps' offered to wedding couples in form of, for example, wedding checklists. The most common paths are well-marked in those; a wedding couple doesn't enter a flat landscape and the keepsake box, which still waits to be filled, also affects the trajectories. Experiences worth remembering and possible to save in some kind of material form has to be created (see 'to-do list'). Even if the box is empty there are expectations of what it will hold in the future.

The becoming of a wedding is a process but on the way certain things have to be more set. You can only marry one person (at one time), wear one dress, one ring and one bouquet. All the other thousand dresses have to be excluded. Some materiality helps to narrow down all the choices, as in the ceremony/dress example.

When the wedding starts to take form – by the reservations, contracts and the things that are purchased along the way – it takes more work to change direction. By the various actors the wedding gets more and more stable. And weddings are much about stability.

The chosen one – the ring pillow, music, cake topping, and invitation cards and so on – will be the treasured result of a whole lot of negotiations. Ultimately the wedding kept in the box will not show signs of the negotiations; it will show the wedding as almost created from above, like if a magic stick had been in work. All the negotiations are stored in the other box, the working material box.

Time to preserve heritage

All the different paths that the wedding potentially could have taken are no longer under negotiation when the wedding morning dawns. One dress has won, one bouquet, one cake, one hair style, one menu and so on. During the wedding day the ideal is to 'go with the flow' but at the same time not to forget the future. At the same time as all the magic feeling should arise, someone has to be rational enough to start preserving memories. For example the chosen bouquet, if it is to be preserved, has to be taken to a florist the very next day, after spending the night in a refrigerator.

Some of the items that will end up in the keepsake box need treatment to be able to keep fresh. They have to be dried, preserved or in other ways conserved. There are things like photos, tickets (paper), laces (fabric) and flowers (dried) that are suggested to be placed in the box. All of this is materiality with lasting qualities, even though nothing ever lasts forever. Materiality that molds, rots, disintegrates or in other ways changes too much won't make it to the keepsake box.

The preservation of a bouquet is a rather complicated process. First the bouquets are documented by taking a picture of it (to help the florist remember how it looked!). Second the flowers are taken apart and then they will be 'dried', and there are several different techniques for this. Some of them involving chemical solutions to: 'hold in color and open the cell structure of the flower. This enhances the water removal process during the freeze-dying process while retaining the flowers' natural color' (www.heelerandreid.com). The decision to preserve a bouquet, might affect the choice of flowers. Some are more difficult to preserve than others. Thick flower stems are more difficult to preserve, there is a risk that they might mold before they dry. Bold colors are said to be easier to keep than pale colors. But some techniques are argued as having the ability to preserve even difficult flowers by using different chemicals: 'Depending on the type and color of the flower, it is treated with one of 14 different solutions' (Ibid). The cost for preservation can be more than the actual bouquet. If a bouquet is too big to fit into our small box, there are specially designed airproof cupboards to keep them in. What I found in my box was a preserved corsage, a small flower arrangement for the groom to wear on his lapel.

Another thing that is too big to end up in the box is the wedding dress, but there are certain kits which include boxes to buy for preserving the dress.

Your exquisite bridal gown is both the focus of your wedding day and the ultimate reflection of your heart, your dreams, your style, your hopes for the future. After the wedding, capture the spirit of this special time by preserving your gown according to archival standards. The Family Jewels Bridal Gown Preservation Box Kit is easy to use, affordable, and the only way to protect your investment. Long after the ceremony is over and your new life has begun, your gown will be a living heirloom, something to be enjoyed time and again, passed on to another bride, or used as part of a christening dress or bassinette (*http://familyjewelsarchival.com/themeweddingdresskit.htm* (2006–10–15)

It is possible to vacuum pack the dress, which one of my transformants told me his wife, had done with her dress, but another way to keep it is to buy the preservation kit presented above. It includes white gloves – in the ad compared to the ones they use at museums – chemical preparations and acid free tissues for wrapping and a box (which can be ordered in three different sizes) (ibid). [6]

In this part of the process of preservation, questions about authenticity start to swirl around in my head. It is obvious, in these ads, that time should leave no traces. What the companies in these cases offer is protection against the ravages of time. The dress and the flowers should look as good as new, even after many years. I can't help to think of items that get its value *because* one can see the age. Does a wedding dress in mint condition improve memories? Or perhaps the expensive dress, $1000 is not unusually, is kept for other reasons than showing authentic wine stains from the wedding party!

My consideration comes from the ideas circling around other items in the box, where traces of the actual wedding are seen as admirable. 'Our wedding, a memory book' (Carter, 1992), is a book that the couple is advised to 'activate' during the wedding day and later on there are frames in the book where pictures should be attached. There are places for the guests to write greetings. Things that are kept, like this book, should ideally evoke feelings that are as authentic as possible. Things collected during the actual day with marks from actual participants, like greetings, contribute to the genuine feeling. There are other ways to get in contact with 'genuine' memories.

6 Fabric is considered as difficult materiality at museums. Some fabric, such as silk, 'destroys' itself over time. Some colors are difficult to preserve. Museums used to have problems displaying textiles at exhibitions. Textiles need to be kept clean, dark, dry and untouched. Sweat, grease from fingers and other bodily fluids ruin the fibers if they are left in the fabrics.

Senses in a box

Different types of materiality are intermixed in the box and different things have different competences in the memory work. Photos, that I will deal with later on, stimulate for example sight and touch. But the other senses: smell, sound and taste should also be activated. If all senses can be stimulated by opening the box, more and stronger memories can be reached. All the senses can be stimulated by opening the box: smell, taste, touch, sight and sound. Sight is the sense that is thought to be closely connected to mind and knowledge. With our eyes we can capture a great range of information. Touch on the other hand has been seen as the sense most closely connected to the body. Touch has a certain position as the 'truth' sense: 'seeing's believing, but touching's the truth' (Korsmeyer, 2004:86). The lack of connection to bodies when we hear and see, continues Korsmeyer, is one reason why these senses appear as more abstract and intellectual. If one longs for true 'flashbacks', taste or smell can be more effective than the 'intellectual' eyes.

That is the market idea of some of the products sold in connection to memories. In the box there is a bottle of perfume. An especially selected perfume from a company that is specialized in selling different commodities to keep memories alive.

> Keep your wedding memories alive... The life invites you to a lot of experience worth remembering. Your wedding is among the most important. Your scent sense bares the key to always remembering this special occasion. Scents have the unique ability to awake and enhance feelings which a memory is made of. The magic feelings that a scent creates goes beyond the ones that photos and other memorabilia can (My translation. http://www.rememberwhen.se/ (2006 – 12 – 06).

Buying a perfume that is only used during the wedding makes the perfume, according to the company that sells it, capable of recreating the 'wonderful feelings that your wedding gave you and immortalizing that magical feeling of love!' (ibid). The names of the scents offered are: dream, bond, caress, float, imagine, inspire, laugh, love, smile, tickle, touch.

The CD in the box contains the couple's special songs that were played at the wedding. They told me that they don't play the songs on the CD very often; they want to keep the songs special. The music should be connected to the wedding and not to other occasions. The perfume and the music shouldn't be overused because they could lose the special connection to the wedding. The box ultimately should be closed and not reopened too often. It's as if the memories can be worn out but at the same time are in need of materiality to maintain alive.

Food is among the materiality that is difficult to keep for a longer period of time. When I looked into my transformants' wedding albums, food is a common subject in the photos. This is one way of remembering taste. Keeping menus or/and recipes in the box is another way. Keeping a piece of the cake or even putting a piece in the freezer and perhaps eating it on an anniversary requires a whole lot of preservatives.

In an earlier quote, a piece of lace is said to bring back memories. Fabrics stimulate tactility but are difficult to handle in the long run. As I have written, the wedding dress can be kept almost like a sacred relict, packed into an acid-free box. It needs a lot of attention to keep fresh. I found other items made of fabric in the box, smaller than and not as expensive as a dress: a small handbag which matched the dress worn at the wedding, a ring pillow, and a pairs of gloves, of course with a special device so that the ring finger easily can be uncovered.

What someone puts into the wedding keepsake box gets personalized and is seldom of any greater interest for others than the ones involved, but the collection in its compositions of different materiality should have the ability to awake sublime feelings or even be magic. Technology – such as freeze-drying, preservationists and digital media – could be seen as instrumental in shaping emotions associated with love and romance (Michael, 2000).

Even if the box is starting to get filled I would like to keep the box open a little bit longer in this chapter. We haven't worked with the photos and the scrapbook, yet.

Wormhole in space-time

A way to make things, such as food, more sustainable and smaller, is to take photos. Photos are the most common memorabilia. Photos can be a way of sharing the wedding experience with others. That might have disqualified photos for being a part of this chapter: a wedding keepsake box can be a private affair which the couple doesn't show in the same way as an album with pictures. The box can also be a place/space, as I stated earlier, that ultimately should be kept closed once it is completed. Photos on the other hand is often showed and shared. However photos, scrapbooks and videos are closely connected with memories and often a part of the stuff put into the box.

Photos are the ultimate 'evidence' of an event. At selected photos, not the failed ones, you see the wedding dress without stains, always on the body that doesn't change. The hairstyle is perfect and the couple's smiles that never faint. Frozen in a split of a second the wedding is perfect. Photos are both a concentration and a way to distribute an event. Photos can be seen as a network which exists highly temporarily and spatially. But during that short moment crystals or pixels has created a structure that can, with work, exist long after the assemblies have disappeared.

The fact that a camera is present and the attention that these moments will be frozen in photography, and maybe glued (with special glue that doesn't affect the photos in a long run, of course) in a scrapbook, does something to the occasions. The idea of an album affects the wedding and creates memories of the wedding in advance.

> 'A Wedding is the most memorable occasion of one's lifetime. Creating a wedding scrapbook is a great idea to keep some of the unforgettable memories of the wedding intact' (*http://www.indianchild.com/wedding/wedding-scrapbook-layouts.htm* (2006 – 12 – 06)).

Photos are light that has been inscribed on a piece of paper or arranged pixels in a camera/computer. In a photo traces of an event are structured, even if it is temporary, in a way which is never achievable for a naked eye to capture. All the details are possible to grasp and return to, over and over again. 'Remember ... It's not thousands words each picture's worth. It's a thousand memories' (Modern Bride, 1992:24).

Those frozen memories are worth attention, work and a nice framing, according to the ads for scrapbooking. Photos can be precious mementos and if the photos are arranged in a scrapbook it can become a hobby involving even more materiality after the wedding.

> 'A wedding scrapbook is not only fun to assemble; it will also be a lasting keepsake for the newlyweds that will remind them of their special day forever. If you are planning on making a wedding scrapbook, start planning the scrapbook well before the wedding, and begin assembly following the actual wedding, when you have accumulated all the photos, mementos, and other special items from the wedding' (http://www.lexmark.com/uncomplicate/ (2006 – 12 – 06)).

In this quote the scrapbook can, just like the box, activate the collecting of material to put into it, it is a process of accumulating an assembly that will become some of the 'evidences' of the wedding. When the wedding is over it's time to work with photos – from the wedding, honeymoon, rehearsal dinner and so on – tickets, engagement and wedding announcement from newspapers, the special imprinted napkins.

Another reason to work with the memorabilia after the wedding can be that the wedding day is usually very hectic. The time-table and logistics can be very tight: some hours at the hair dresser's to get the hair done and to get dressed, then some time with a photographer before the ceremony, then to the reception. Some of the people I have talked to about their wedding day say they didn't have time or the nerve to actually experience and feel anything during the day. The feelings you should have felt can instead be achieved through work with the photos, memory books and when taking care of the items that are to be kept. The nice feelings and the 'flow' can be created in the album, felt during the preparation of a scrapbook but weren't perhaps felt during the actual wedding day. [7]

There is no end to what a scrapbook can cost in money and time. There are special wedding accessories sold to create a scrapbook: stamps, paper, pearls, glitter, stickers and so on. The mementos are combined with these accessories to create nice pages. Weddings are appreciative events to work around. There are certain symbols that are recurring: cakes (in many layers), rings, hearts, champagne bottles and glasses and of course heterosexual couples in all sizes and styles. The fact that those symbols are the ones sold to enthusiastic scrap-bookers who want to craft weddings, make them a 'must' and a norm at a wedding.

Never made scrapbooking? Don't worry, there are classes you can attend. I interviewed a lady that owns a scrapbooking shop and arranges classes for learning how to make nice pages. She told me that it is very common that newly weds (brides) [8] attend her workshops. A wedding can be a good excuse to broaden your horizons in various ways.

When the scrapbook is finished we can show it to friends and relatives for a while, but sooner or later it probably will end up in the keepsake box. Some photos will be framed and put on the wall or on a piano at the homes of friends and family members. Now, the box is about to get closed.

---

7 In Nita Rollins article: *Something Borrowed, Something Taped: Video Nuptials* she writes about an documentary entitled 'How to Shoot A Wedding' and among the tips she finds the suggestion that: 'footage of the seated guests awaiting the wedding ceremony might be "cut in" later as reaction shots for significant moments' (Rollins, 1991:37). An admirable narrative can be created afterwards.

8 A gender perspective on mementos, gift giving and weddings is of course very interesting (Di Leonardo, 1987: Otnes & Pleck, 2003). But the perspective in this chapter doesn't deal with that, even though that would have added even more angles to the subject.

Time capsule

Some of the things in the keepsake box challenge the borders of the box, like scrapbooks which are more official and public then other things in it. The box has four walls, a bottom and a lid. It's a small territory where time, and by that changeability, should be kept outside. Time ought to pass by without affecting the content and the memories stored in the box. If the things in the box succeed the moments will stay forever in the hearts of the couple, if one believes the ad. If one doesn't trust the box there are 'time capsules' to buy:

> The Wedding Time Capsule Set is perfect for the Bride and Groom to fill with keepsake memorabilia from their wedding day, honeymoon and first year together. This magical Time Capsule is then sealed until a special anniversary in the future (www:Bridalpeople.com/memory. 2006 – 12 – 01).

The box or 'time capsule' can be seen as a territory of security, a space and place where it is possibly to have control (see also Mörck in this volume) as long as time in the shape of a decade is kept outside. A 'time capsule' produces certainty and all the translations that have preceded the content are hidden and in the 'time capsule' things are put out of reach and are no longer possible to renegotiate. A 'time capsule' is actually sealed, just like a can of beans.

The experience of time is strange; we can't explain or define our experience of it. We often use metaphors like: time goes; time flies and time runs out. We can speak of a torrent of time that seems to have one direction and that is toward a future.

Knowledge can reach us from the past but not from the future. Time seems to have a one-way direction and it is irreversible. This understanding of time is similar to that of distance i.e. distance is the space between two points and time is the distance between two events, this is a static way of thinking of time and space. If the world is pictured as a fixed set of beings to which our feelings and memories reflects like a snapshot, then the narrative is closed and not capable of an open becoming. (De Landa, 1999).

If time instead is seen as a multiplicity of times constructed in loose, dynamic networks of intertwined and mangled assemblies (Deleuze, 1992; Kavanagh and Araujo, 1995; Pickering, 1993), it is possible to analyze a wedding keepsake box as a temporal and local zone where motions are slowed down. A time capsule where the assemblies try to prevent others, and time, to 'invade the setting and interrupting its existence' (Akrich and Latour, 2000 (1992:261).

The assembly – the box and everything it contains – is considered as 'being' and not 'becoming' (see also Johansson in this volume) as if that was possible. And perhaps it is in some sense, but even what appears as beings are always in motion at some level. In the box much effort is made to prevent motion even at a microscopically level – by using acid-free papers and chemical substances for preservation. – but sooner or later the content will disintegrate. Permanence costs a lot and requires many allies. Stability can only be local and never 'forever'.

The items in a wedding keepsake box are not only representations or symbols, they *do* something. The ads and texts encouraging the purchase of these boxes use arguments that feel very familiar to me, stating that there are no clear boundaries between mind, body and materiality. We constantly use competence around us and the relative durability of the materiality in the box is given the competence to remembering. Action is often seen as a human property but if society consisted simply of associations of humans, then social order would rest on face-to-face situation. Agency is not the sole privilege of humans but can also reside in non-humans, such as a keepsake box (Latour, 1999).

Even if the box in the end is counted as one it is made out of countless parts. The box is full of technique, chemicals, know-how and a lot of different molecule structures, in other words a lot of humans and non-humans have been involved in the process of making and closing the box. And when the box finally is closed it has become mobile thanks to the stability and relatively small size. The wedding becomes both distributed and closed at the same time. The wedding and the memories of it have become 'white boxed'.

Creation and Transformation of Value

Karin M. EKSTRÖM

Introduction

It is perfectly silent in a room filled with people and the auctioneer welcomes everybody to this year's art glass auction. All the seats are occupied and some people who have not been able to find seats are standing at the back, close to the entrance. It feels as if the atmosphere is filled with expectations, curiosity and concentration. Some of these people have been looking forward to this event all year. The auctioneer says that there will be an extraordinary amount of telephone bids [1] this year, a coffee break in the middle of the auction as usual, and he also explains where the objects can be paid for and fetched after the auction. Then, he proceeds by asking cheerfully if there is anyone who does not know the rules regarding the premium to be paid in connection with a purchase. No one answers and the auction can begin.

The setting for this chapter is a high quality art glass auction held on Sunday afternoon, the 6th of August 2006, at Kosta glass factory in Småland, Sweden. Småland is a province where most of the glass in Sweden has been produced historically. The art glass auction is a yearly event held in cooperation with Stockholm Auction House and Orrefors Kosta Boda. This year, the 21st time the auction is held, is special in that a complete glass collection is sold. The collection includes 65 art glass objects, representing the development of Swedish art glass during the 20th century. The 20th century was a time when the Swedish glass industry flourished and received international recognition. Phillips (1987:224) writes, '...when Swedish glass was shown to the world at the Paris Exhibition in 1925, it became clear to everyone that a new nation had entered the world of fine glassmaking.' Swedish glass also received recognition during the World exhibition in New York 1939, when the concept 'Swedish Modern' was established (Huldt, 1999). The demand for Swedish art glass increased significantly after the Second World War and became an essential international profile for Swedish design during the 1950s (e.g., Sandon, 1999)

---

1 Telephone bids make it possible for an interested potential buyer to bid through a representative at the auction house, under the condition that telephone lines are available. The number of telephone bids has increased over the years and is used by interested potential buyers from Sweden and abroad.

People waiting in line to attend the auction
Photographer: Karin M. Ekström

The purpose of this chapter is to discuss creation and transformation of value of art glass objects focusing on the auction, and in particular the glass collection sold. It is of interest to identify different and multiple meanings of value(s) created and transformed by the persons selling and buying, collectors and non-collectors, but also the auction company, Stockholm Auction House, and the people observing the event. By contrasting different experiences and relations to glass objects including the collection sold, we may better understand the multiple meanings of value (s). ANT (Actor Network theory) is used here to illustrate the creation and transformation of value(s) in a network consisting of people and artifacts at the auction. Below follows a description of value(s), a discussion of how ANT is used in this specific setting, a presentation of the auction, the collection sold and different interpretations of how value(s) are created and transformed at the auction.

The multidimensional and elusive meaning of value(s)

The meaning of value is often vaguely defined, both in written and spoken word. From an economic perspective, it is the *economic value or exchange value* which often comes to mind. It represents the value determined by the market, in this case the auction, where objects are sold and bought. This resembles what Lai (1995:384) defines as *customer value*, namely, 'the buyer's evaluation at the time of a product purchase'. According to Urban and Hauser (1993:213), customer value is '...the tradeoff between the benefits of a product and the price paid.' This definition implies that the customer will choose the product with the most utility per money paid. At the auction, a potential buyer will continue to bid until he/she feels the price is higher than the benefits received. For example, a collector told me after the art glass auction that he really liked an old overlay vase. The estimated price was 12,000 – 15,000 SEK and it was sold for 18,500 SEK, a price he considered too high so he stopped bidding.

For both the economic, exchange and customer value, the focus is on the purchasing moment. It is the outcome rather than the process of creating and transforming value which is the center of attention. However, a person bidding at the auction is likely to carry thoughts from the past as well as expectations regarding the future, both regarding the benefits of the product and the price paid, into the decision-making process. For example, several glass collectors I previously interviewed have referred to childhood memories from the glass factories in Småland (Ekström, 2004). The economic value only accounts for a restricted part of the multi-dimensional meaning of value, in that the focus is on the monetary appraisal of what something is worth. Other determining aspects of value such as affective value and historical value are out of sight behind the more visible monetary representation.

The *affective value* represents the buyer's evaluation of his/her sentiments towards an object. A product with little or no economic value can have very high affective value, or vice versa. A glass vase with jagged edges can have a strong personal meaning for someone, but may be impossible to sell at an auction. Also, a person investing in glass objects for speculation can be willing to pay a very high price, but feel detached to the objects. Since Swedish prices on art glass have fluctuated over the years, it is possible that an investor who is taking a high financial risk may also want to feel some emotional attachment to the object, in case it will be impossible to sell the object for some period of time. This is an argument I have heard antique dealers use when discussing antiques in general. Also, products representing visual consumption such as glass objects may by design involve some affective value. This, however, does not imply that products involving less visual consumption have less affective value.

Another value related to the affective value is *the nostalgic value*. It represents a yearning to return to an earlier time which can be reinforced by a purchase. For example, a collector's purchase of glass produced during his/her childhood can signify recollections and longing for the past. A person I previously interviewed collects glass specifically produced at Pukeberg glass factory where his father worked and where he himself also started working when he was twelve years old during his summer and Christmas vacations (Ekström, 2004). Nostalgia can also be an expression of shared societal values during a specific period. A collector of glass from the 1950s who I previously interviewed talked about the progress in society, reflected in architecture, art and glass, during that decade (Ekström, 2004). Furthermore, collector's engagements are sometimes perceived as noble in that they take care of things other people throw away, only a few people appreciate or things museums cannot maintain. To 'save' art glass for future generations can represent *noble value*.

The historical value represents an appraisal of the past. In this chapter, it is manifested in the location of the auction, Kosta glass factory in Småland. Sweden has had a large number of glass factories during the 20th century, a majority of them situated in the southern province Småland. Examples of glass factories in Småland which are internationally well-known are Orrefors, Kosta, Boda [2] and Åfors. Previous interviews with glass collectors have shown their interest to search for and find the origin of their objects, involving relations to the designers and trying to identify glass workers who have created the glass (Ekström 2004). At the auction, a ravenna bowl, number 274 from the collection to be sold, is for sale. It is a very special ravenna, a double ravenna in blue and red, designed by Sven Palmqvist in 1969, the same year as the designer's son Petter Palmqvist got engaged, according to the curator at Stockholm Auction House, Ulrika Ruding. The estimated price is 10,000SEK-12,000SEK and it is later sold for 13,500SEK. To know an object's origin, *provenance*, commonly adds to the value among collectors as well as non-collectors.

The historical value is also manifested in that the Stockholm Auction House's art glass auction is always held in Småland where most of the glass has been and still is produced. The room where this year's auction is held is

[2] Kosta and Boda are glass factories at two different locations even though the companies merged some years ago. Orrefors and Kosta-Boda are today owned by the same company, New Wave Group AB.

normally a glass house, but is transformed into an auction hall when the auction is held. The exterior and interior clearly show this. It was noticeable the first day the glass objects were on display that the glass house was very hot, since the ovens which normally produce glass in the same room had not cooled down. The annual event of transforming a glass house into an auction brings excitement and *experiential value*. The experiential aspects of consumption (e.g., Holbrook and Hirschman, 1982) are strong among people attending an auction to observe, bid and purchase glass objects. An example is my observation of a family who stayed at the same hotel as I did. The couple had brought their children and their spouses to Kosta for the auction. I noticed them later at the auction both observing the objects on display during the show and attending the auction. In retrospect, the experiential value changes and seems more closely linked to the memory of the experience than the particular experience in itself. A collector I previously interviewed emphasized the social dimension of collecting when visiting auctions, 'You meet a lot of people who you have not seen for many years at auctions. It is like one big social reunion' (Ekström, 2004). The social aspect was also noticeable when Konst- och Bruksglasföreningen, a glass-collecting society, traditionally met at the auction hall the day before the auction, to be shown the objects on display exclusively by the curator Ulrika Ruding.

It is interesting to reflect upon the *agency of value*. The economic and exchange value are by definition determined by the market, implying the seller and the buyer. The creation and transformation of value are also influenced by the cultural context. Miller (2000: 78) states, 'value is not something that the exchanged objects are reduced to, but something created by the act itself. The implication of such studies is that the definition of value varies according to the context of transaction.' The agency of value rests for the customer value, the affective value and the nostalgic value mostly on the buyer, although not solely. Value is determined in a cultural context involving both societal values and social expectations. A collector creates value by producing his/her collection, but also producing him/herself as a collector.

It should also be noticed that products are not only given value by sellers and buyers, but value is produced by the product itself. For example, a product with wear and tear may represent damage and diminished value, but also be perceived as having beautiful patina. *Patina* is the surface appearance of something grown beautiful with age or use. The interpretation of patina is likely to vary depending on society and time as well as the buyer's interpretation of how it benefits the object's appearance. Ocular inspection of wear and tear can show a product's function and usage (e.g., Bringéus 1986). Different ways to repair a product can also show how it has been valued in the past (e.g., Bringéus 1986). A product's *functional value* or *use value* may, however, not necessarily show the meaning it may have for a consumer. Instead it may show how the product is intended to be used from the designer's perspective which does not necessarily correspond with the consumer's perspective. Previous interviews with art glass collectors have made me realize that they are very conscious about the fact that water can produce limestone spots. Therefore, they prefer not to use their vases. A collector said that some persons are surprised that the vases he collects cannot be used, "... they wonder why we have a difficult time finding vases when someone graduates from high school, for example. There are several hundreds, but we cannot pour water into any of them" (Ekström, 2004).

A value is also appropriated by the owner from the time it is purchased until it is disposed of. The appropriation process consists of different rituals such as possession, grooming and exchange rituals (e.g., McCracken, 1986; Östergaard, Fitchett and Jantzen 1999). Interviews with glass collectors have previously shown how they spend time dusting and arranging their collections (e.g., Ekström, 2005). The *display value* reflects, but is also influenced by, how objects are valued by its owner. A glass object which is perceived as important to someone is commonly given a prominent place in the home. Also, treasured glass objects are displayed in the catalogue as well as in glass cabinets to be examined when they are on display before the auction starts. Collections are perceived differently depending on if they are displayed symmetrically, asymmetrically, horizontally in the entire room or vertically in shelves or cupboards (e.g., Belk et al., 1988). The composition and creativity involved in arranging collections are important to recognize in the process of how value is created.

The relation between value and values

The intertwined relation between value and values needs to be recognized. Depicting value as objectified and values as subjectified is much too simplified. Both value and values are related to meanings, experiences, relations and negotiations. They are intermingled in that value affects values and values affect value. Value is created by people in their experiences, relations and negotiations with other people and artifacts. Values are both the product and the process of living in a cultural context. Miller (2000) has highlighted the need to scrutinize the relationship between exchange and value, between market variables such as price and equivalence and the attributes of something, what really matters to us. Lai (1995:384) distinguishes customer value, discussed above, from *consumer values*. He defines the latter as "people's valuation of product consumption or possession." Different *product benefits* have also been referred to as consumption values by Sheth, Newman, and Gross (1991). They distinguish the difference between functional, social, emotional, epistemic, and conditional benefits. Lai (1995) prefers to call them generic product benefits which a consumer can obtain from possession or consumption and distinguishes between eight of these: functional, social, affective, epistemic, aesthetic, hedonic, situational and holistic. Different buyers, both individual and antique dealers, are likely to experience different benefits from purchasing art glass at the auction.

The fact that the products we possess influence our self-image has by Belk (1988) been defined as the *extended self*. Things are also instrumental for developing our self-image (Belk, 1988). Owning precious art glass can make a person feel great. There are strong relations between a collector and a collection. Is it the collector who collects the items collected or the other way around (Ekström, 2004)? Losing a collection can be perceived as losing a part of one's identity. I once met a man who sadly talked about when his collection of cups was stolen. A person who enjoys having things, allowing himself/herself to become attached to things shows a willingness to have relations, both to things and other people. Latour (1998, 1999) emphasizes that actants; humans and non-humans, are given agency in relation to other actants. In fiction, collectors are sometimes described as anti-social, but my impression is that they often are very social, interacting not only with their collections, but with other collectors on the Internet, in collector's clubs, at auctions and fairs. To find and acquire objects for a collection usually requires social connections. Miller (1998) writes about how a person without things can show an inability to create relations. Also, Baudrillard (1996) discusses the importance of social connections.

The *symbolic meaning* of products has earlier been emphasized by Hirschman and Holbrook (1982). McCracken (1988) discusses how the culture sets the context that provides symbols meaning. In Sweden, glass is often considered to be a part of the Swedish soul. The meaning of glass produced in Småland is for a Swede in general different than glass produced in China.

ANT, value(s) and the auction

The Actor Network Theory (ANT) is expected to benefit the understanding of value(s), recognizing the multidimensional aspects and also recognizing how the creation and transformation of value are influenced by the cultural context. ANT also makes it possible to understand the relations between value and values. For the emergence of value, the place where something is bought is just as important as the items bought (Miller, 2000). In this chapter, the high quality glass auction is essential for the people attending and purchasing glass. The auction company is a nexus where people and things are linked to each other in different ways. The personnel's expertise is connected so that one person's knowledge in one area is complemented by someone else's expertise in another area. Knowledge is also exchanged among people attending the auction who learn from each other discussing particular objects for sale, but also among the personnel and people attending the auction, who learn from each other. An interesting object for sale at this year's auction is number 8 from 1914 – 1916, a pink and purple overlay vase with green trees bearing fruit. It is signed Orrefors HW (the subject engraved by Heinrich Wallman) and a copy of the original drawing is attached to the vase, signed by Fritz Blomqvist. The collectors, Witting-Eklund, described below, selling the vase had found the drawing in the Orrefors archive. This is an example of when collectors provide the auctioneering company as well as the audience knowledge. Knowledge can be considered a resource in the ANT network.

Agency is given as a consequence of the relation in the particular location. A collector at the auction is perceived as a connoisseur, but may in another context be seen as an amateur. The framing is in this chapter the auction, mainly the actual event during the Sunday afternoon, but also the two days preceding the auction when the objects have been on display for viewing. This framing allows us to analyze what happens at the auction, but it gives us no insight into what is going on in people's homes before or after the auction. However, previous interviews with collectors (Ekström, 2004) have given some information of what goes on before and after actions. For example, the implicit prescription that art glass vases should not be used to hold flowers (water can produce limestone spots), as discussed above. The process of translation is illustrated in how objects are moved during the auction and given a special position on a pedestal during the bidding. It is also reflected in how objects are moved from someone's home to the auction and the back into someone else's home.

Inspired by Latour (1999) and Law (1991), the auction is perceived as a monster[3] that exists in a network of different actors, being the people observing, bidding, buying, the personnel at the auction house, the magnificent glass objects for sale, the auction catalogue and the bidding paddles. The monster transforms glass objects into different dimensions of value(s). An auction can turn commodities into sacred collectibles (Belk, 1995). The people selling and buying and the personnel at the auction company can be seen as mediators or translators transforming different dimensions of value(s). Different intermediaries are also used such as the glossy auction catalogue, the bidding paddle[4] described below, and of course money which is highly noticeable, but not visible, in a prominent auction like the one studied.

The individual glass objects can also be seen as little monsters being fragile entities displayed attractively in glass cabinets when on view before the auction, or placed on a pedestal throughout the silent bidding during the auction. Different trajectories are constructed when ordering the little monsters in glass cupboards when on view. This year's auction is different in that the little monsters are displayed according to color rather than according to designer, as in previous years. Trajectories are also assembled in the auction catalogue where the little monsters are listed according to designers, except for this year's collection to be sold, numbered 1 – 65, including a variety of designers at the beginning of the catalogue.

Another example of trajectories constructed is when the little monsters are moved to and from the pedestal for the treasured moments of silent bidding. The trajectories also include embedded rituals involving dusting of the glass objects and placing them in attractive positions, either as a glorious single little monster or next to other little monsters. The latter with the intention of sparking magnificent luster on each other, adds value, but at the same time runs the risk of dissipating interest from one another. The placement, either in the glass cabinets or in the catalogue is likely to affect the transformation of value. For example, if a precious little monster is placed next to a little monster considered valueless by a viewer, the former may be considered even more precious and the latter even more worthless, or the opposite. This discussion can also be applied to individual glass objects, little monsters, in people's homes. Previous interviews with collectors have shown that such little monsters are often

3 Monster is our playful name for the commercial culture assemblages framed in this book, highlighting their hybrid and mixed character bridging culture-economy, everyday culture-commerce and production-consumption divides.

4 The so-called paddle is a card, as shown in the photo on page 117.

The auction catalogue
Photographer: Ulrika Ruding

A bidding paddle
Photographer: Ulrika Ruding

displayed in appealing ways, paying particular attention to the lightening and removal of dust (e.g., Ekström, 2004).

The auction

The glass auction is a 'silent auction', only the auctioneer's voice is heard. People who bid show a bidding paddle to the auctioneer and telephone bids are signaled by waving hands from the Client Services. Those who want to participate by bidding in the sales room have collected a numbered bidding paddle from the Auction's Client Services prior to the auction. Those who want to bid by telephone should make a request in writing to Client Services no later than one day before the auction. Also, absentee bids instructed in writing should be received by Client Services in Kosta no later than 4 pm the day before the auction. Client Services will then execute bids on behalf of the client and buy at the lowest price possible as allowed by other bids and reserves. In order to bid, whether to choose paddle bidding, telephone bidding or absentee bids, some form of identification or reference is requested by Client Services. Regarding telephone bidding, the Client Services will telephone the client when the bidding is about to start for a specific object. The client can then bid through the representative under the condition that telephone lines are available. Normally, bids will be increased according to the following scale: SEK 200 – 1,000 (minimum increase 50 SEK), 1,000 – 5,000 SEK (min. increase 100 SEK), 5,000 – 10,000 SEK (min. increase 200 SEK), 10,000 – 20,000 SEK (min. increase 500 SEK), 20,000 – 50,000 SEK (min. increase 1,000 SEK), 50,000 – 100,000 SEK (min. increase 2,000 SEK). For each object sold, a premium of 20 percent including VAT on the hammer price[5] plus a hammer fee of SEK 40 is added.

The objects for sale are displayed for viewing the entire day Friday and Saturday as well as Sunday morning prior to the auction which starts at 1 pm. As mentioned above, they are displayed very nicely according to colors in different glass cabinets. The room where they are displayed is the glass factory room which is converted into a sales room at 11 am on Sunday, two hours before the auction starts. Three glass vases with beautiful sunflowers and gladiolus add a nice atmosphere to the room.

[5] The price the auctioneer determines as the last price by using a hammer.

Selling a collection

The collection to be sold at the auction, is a relatively small collection considering the number of items collected, 65 items in total. If taking into account the economic value of the items, it is, however, a relatively large collection. The individual objects in the collection are unique and generate interest among many potential buyers. The items in the collection were produced between 1898 and 1996, with about half of the items produced before the 1950s and the other half after the 1950s. In other words, the collection is an exposé of Swedish art glass from the beginning and throughout the 1900s.

The collection belongs to the couple Maja Witting and Harald Eklund. They started collecting relatively late in life, after they had retired in 1989, because they wanted to find an interest that they shared. Collecting art glass then became their common interest. It comes to my mind that it must be difficult to let go of a collection. The curator, Ulrika Ruding says: '... both Maja and Harald were here yesterday and they said that they still have glass in their hearts, but they have let go of it in a material sense. They will always carry it with them'. In other words, even though they have sold the glass, it still remains with them to some extent. Maybe it is easier to sell a collection which is relatively young? Ulrika Ruding says: '... I can understand that it can be difficult to sell a collection. This collection is only 15 – 20 years old. It is not very old. It might be more difficult to sell a collection which is even older. They thought it was better to sell now and in some way I as a person would think that it is more fun when you can take part and influence a little'. By influence she means that the collectors in cooperation with Stockholm Auction House have written the preface to the catalogue. It is interesting when collectors themselves can personally describe the items to be sold. To know where a collection or items in a collection originate from is something of interest to potential buyers. As mentioned earlier, to know the history of the item, often referred to as provenance, is a dimension of value, which also positively affects the economic value in most cases.

The collectors', Witting's and Eklund's, interest for glass has developed over the years. They have increased their knowledge and conducted research on the Swedish art glass. This has resulted in three publications. [6] Collectors do

6 'Fritz Blomqvist – en nästan bortglömd pinonjär i Glasriket' [Fritz Blomqvist – a nearly forgotten pioneer in the Glass Empire], 'Det tunnväggiga graal-glaset. Signeringar, upphovsmannaskap och droit de suite' [The thin-walled graal glass. Signs, copyright and droit de suite] and 'Graalglaset i konstglaslitteraturen. Om behovet av fortsatta studier och nya texter' [Graal glass in art glass literature. About needs for future studies and new literature].

often have knowledge about things which are not documented anywhere else. Ulrika Ruding says: '... they (the couple Witting-Eklund) have conducted research about this designer Fritz Blomqvist and found out that he is more than just a designer who does his job. It has resulted in that he has become upgraded at the auctions and now received designer status, and this is because of them'. The fact that knowledge is important to collectors is also something interviews with other glass collectors have confirmed (e.g., Ekström 2004). For example, a typical glass collector was described as follows: 'You have to obtain knowledge, you cannot just buy glass and glass, but you have to understand and learn about different types of glass to really enjoy your collecting' (Ekström, 2004). Ulrika Ruding also states that the audience at this type of art glass auction is very knowledgeable: '... at every show before the auction, we learn more and more'. Interviews with other collectors have showed that as knowledge increases, the demand for quality increases. The collection sold was overall of high quality and included a variety of techniques such as 'overlay glass from the turn of the 2000s century, early graal glass, ravenna, kraka, ariel and 'slipgraal' (grinded graal, i.e., a variation of graal glass). Ulrika Ruding says that there is a higher demand for perfect glass at auctions nowadays. Buyers are not interested in defective glass, probably because the economic value is significantly reduced.

It is common that collectors think about how collections should continue to exist after they have passed away (e.g., Belk, 1995). Collections arouse feelings, take time, responsibility and place and it is therefore not obvious that they will stay within the family. It is, however, relatively uncommon that a collection is sold when the collector is still alive. A collection is often seen as part of a collector's identify (e.g., Belk, 1988 etc). To sell a collection can involve difficulties of separation. When a collection is going to be sold, it is however rarely sold at once. There might be several reasons for this. First of all, a collection can be scattered since family members may want to keep some items and sell the rest. Second, even if it is decided that the entire collection will be sold, it may be difficult to obtain a good price for all the individual items at the same occasion. This is particularly the case if the items collected are identical or similar to each other, unless the items are extremely attractive to a large number of potential buyers. Therefore, collections are often sold piece by piece at different occasions.

Observing the auction process

The auction starts just after 1 pm and goes on to just before 6 pm. It is a very warm summer day outdoors, as well as in the sales room. Most people stay for the entire auction even though a few people leave before the break, some more during the break and a few towards the end of the auction. According to Ulrika Ruding, it is very unlikely that an audience stays for such a long period of time at other quality auctions normally held in Stockholm. As mentioned above, many people has come to bid, but some also visit the auction to observe the event. A trend is that the auction attracts more foreign buyers and it was also noticeable at this year's auction according to Ulrika Ruding.

There is a long line outside the sales room before it is opened to the public. The sales room fills up almost immediately after opening the doors – 15 minutes before the auction begin. People can choose to sit either on a platform or along the side of a room. When you sit on the platform, you have the best view of the screen where the objects to be sold are shown (via a projector), the auctioneer, persons handling the telephone bids and also the audience (you can see who bids). The advantage of sitting on the long side is that you can see the objects for sale on view better before it is auctioneered, showed by the personnel and also placed on a pedestal during the bidding. The audience consists of a few more men than women and it seems as if the majority of the audience is middle-age or above. Even though the audience consists of both men and women, it is apparent that it is mainly men who bid and walk over to the cashier to pay for the objects bought. Erika Lagerbielke, the famous glass designer, is also part of the audience during the first part of the auction. Three of the objects for sale at the auction are designed by her.

Apart from the auctioneer, there are five persons handling the telephone bids, two persons handling the Client services (one of them controlling the absentee bids and the other one handling the cashier for people wanting to pay and fetch items purchased). In addition, there are two persons showing the items to the audience and thereafter placing it on a pedestal during the bidding. It should be added that most people bidding have probably observed the objects carefully prior to the auction when they are on view. I suspect impulse purchases to be rare at this type of auction with high-priced items.

The personnel are all dressed in nice clothes. The auctioneer who came from Stockholm the evening prior to the auction in shorts has now transformed into a black suit. People in the audience chat a little with each other before the auction starts. The man sitting next to me on the platform says to his neighbor that he is from a larger town about an hour away and has come just to observe. It seems as if there are many people who have come just to observe. The auction is a performance (e.g., Goffman, 1959/1990). In the audience, I notice some of the collectors I have interviewed a couple of years ago, who then mentioned the auction as being a special event each year.

There are technical problems before the auction begins. The remote control used for showing the pictures of the objects on the screen does not work. A person in the audience who speaks English comes over to talk to the personnel and explains what he thinks the reason could be. It is probably the iron row next to the platform which causes the problem. It is solved by giving the remote control to one of the persons who handles the telephone bids. He manages to do this throughout the entire auction, except for a couple of times when he handles a telephone bid himself and does not manage to show the picture until the end of the bid.

During the auction the bidding paddles go up and down and the auction moves along quickly. The auction proceeds rapidly, you have to react fast and take down the paddle quickly in order not to be perceived as a continuous bidder by the auctioneer. Suddenly, a buyer is holding his paddle upside down. The number reads 1906 and the auctioneer asks the buyer to turn the paddle so that it reads 9061. Before the auction started, I acquired a bidding paddle myself, to be able to experience the feeling of it. I had seen a very nice glass object and thought that if it is offered at an inexpensive price, I might use the paddle. It never happened, since the price for the very nice glass object immediately rose to a very high level. It was, however, very exciting seconds in a researcher's life.

A woman and two teenage girls, at least one being her daughter, are sitting in front of me. The girls talk to the woman sometimes, but she is very reserved not to disturb. The girls want her to purchase some objects. At one occasion, the daughter says: "mom, can't you buy this, my birthday is coming up soon". The mother does not react. During the break, I join some of the collectors I have previously interviewed and they generously share their thoughts regarding the objects sold as well as the prices. The auction continues after the break and it is fascinating to see all the people engaged by silently observing or bidding. The atmosphere is positive up until the very end and I am impressed by the auctioneer's ability to concentrate and perform throughout the entire afternoon.

Sold and unsold objects in the collection

The estimated price for this year's auction is 2.5 million SEK and the price stops at 3 million SEK, including the collection as well as other glass objects sold. Both sellers and Stockholm Auction House could feel pleased. The collection is sold for 834,000 SEK. Several of the items in the collection such as art glass designed by Fritz Blomqvist, Edvin Öhrström, Sven Palmqvist, Nils Landberg, Kjell Engman and Ann Wolff are sold for much more than the estimated price.

The interest in Fritz Blomqvist's overlay vase from Orrefors, number 8 in the collection, is large and results in the highest price (57,000 SEK) over the estimated price (25,000 – 30,000 SEK). It is the vase, described above, having the original drawing attached to it, which the collectors, Witting-Eklund, had found in Orrefors archive.

As mentioned above, a yearly tradition is that Konst- och Bruksglasföreningen, a glass collecting society, meet the day before the auction to be shown the objects on display exclusively by the Stockholm Auction House's curator Ulrika Ruding. Her stories about the objects add an extra dimension to the pleasure of viewing the art glass. Some examples of stories related to the collection to be sold are presented here. For example, Ulrika Ruding says that number 21, a Fishgraal bowl by Edward Hald from 1937, is a very good object if someone is interested in starting a collection of graal glass. The estimated price is 8,000 – 10,000 SEK and it is later sold for 6,500 SEK. The story about object number 8 was mentioned earlier. Another object from the collection sold is number 28, a bowl in pâte-de-verre technique from 1925, designed by Agnes de Frumerie. This bowl was refused at the World exhibition in Stockholm 1936. The estimated price is 8,000 – 10,000 SEK and it is later sold for 7,000 SEK. Two ravenna bowls are also pointed out by Ulrika Ruding. One of them, number 274, was discussed above. The other ravenna bowl, number 39 from the collection to be sold, a bowl designed by Sven Palmqvist at Orrefors in 1948, the décor being dark read leafs with blue spots. The color combination is unusual and the ravenna is made by crushed rather than powdered color. The estimated price is 18,000 – 20.000 SEK and it is later sold for 37,000 SEK, as a result of many telephone bids.

Only four of the 65 items are not sold. These objects are a few months later, in the beginning of November, offered for sale at the Modern Art and Works of Art Auction held by Stockholm Auction House. It is number 3, an overlay vase, probably designed by Karl Lindeberg, Kosta, but having a later signature from Eda Glass factory. The estimated price at the art glass auction is 12,000 –

15,000 SEK and the highest bid 9,500 SEK, an unaccepted bid according to the collectors selling it (the lower limit for a sale is determined before the auction). The new estimated price for this vase, number 484, at the Modern Art and Works of Art Auction, is 8,000 – 10,000 SEK and it is sold for 7,000 SEK. Also, number 7, an overlay vase designed by Axel Enoch Boman, Reijmyre 1918 remains unsold at the art glass auction (estimated price is 20,000 – 25,000 SEK and highest bid is 13,500SEK). The new estimated price for this vase, number 487, at the Modern Art and Works of Art Auction, is 12,000 – 15,000 SEK and it is sold for 10,000 SEK. Furthermore, number 11, a graal vase, produced in Orrefors 1916 – 1917 is not sold at the art glass auction (estimated price is 12,000 – 15,000 SEK and the highest bid is 9,500 SEK). It is also offered for sale later at the Modern Art and Works of Art Auction (number 486, new estimated price 10 – 12,000 SEK), but remains unsold. Finally, number 18, an engraved bowl from Kosta, signed by Karl Hultström is not sold at the art glass auction (estimated price 8,000 – 10,000 SEK and the highest bid being 6,200 SEK). It is also offered for sale later at the Modern Art and Works of Art Auction (number 494, new estimated price 6,000 – 8,000 SEK), but remains unsold.

Value(s) created and transformed in the auction

I meet a collector couple I previously interviewed (Ekström, 2004), when Ulrika Ruding describes the items for sale to the glass society. They tell me that they are selling two items at the auction. One object is a glass sculpture designed by Ulrika Hydman-Vallien at Kosta. They bought it at an inexpensive price at another auction ten years ago, since they got excited to bid, influenced by others. When I interviewed them previously they discussed how easy it is to get enthusiastic at an auction and how you get influenced to bid by others (Ekström, 2004). The wife said: 'It becomes a psychological game.' The husband said that auctions are ravishing and that it can result in that they avoid auctions. He said that if you are at an auction and no one bids on an object, then it is easy to start bidding, thereafter other people start bidding and then you are involved in the process of bidding (Ekström, 2004). The reason for selling the glass sculpture is that they have recently bought another object at a gallery and discovered that the sculpture took too much room in their home. The estimated price for the glass sculpture is 15,000 – 18,000 SEK. The first bid is 12,500 executed by Client Services and the final price is 15,000 SEK, sold to someone in the room. I also notice that all seven objects designed by Ulrika Hydman-

Vallien on sale at the auction are sold to the same buyer, a young buyer in the room. Maybe he is a collector, an agent buying for someone or a glass dealer? We will never know.

The other object is a so-called tulip glass designed by Nils Landberg, Orrefors. Tulip glasses are today attractive collectibles. The couple bought it with the intention to acquire several tulip glasses, but it never happened. Tulip glasses have gone up in price since they bought theirs. For the last year, it has been stored in a cupboard. The estimated price is 12,000 – 15,000 SEK. The first bid is 10,500 SEK executed by Client Services and the final price 15,000 SEK, a telephone bid executed by Client services. In total, 11 tulip glasses are sold at the auction with prices ranging from 3,000 SEK to 31,000 SEK. Before starting to sell the fragile tulip glasses, the auctioneer says cheerfully: 'we who are going to pack these, hope they get sold'. The person buying the couple's tulip glass buys also another glass for 18,500 SEK (estimated price 12,000 – 15,000 SEK), as well as the most expensive tulip glass for 31,000 SEK (estimated price 12,000 – 15,000 SEK), all sold by telephone bid [7]. When the third glass is sold to him/her, the auctioneer said: 'sold to a collector'. Did the auctioneer know it is a collector? Or did he assume that it is a collector, since all three objects are purchased by the same person? It is also interesting to notice that an English speaking bidder in the auction is bidding on the last tulip glass, but giving up at 31,000 SEK. Instead he buys the next tulip glass for sale for 21,000 SEK (estimated price 12,000 – 15,000 SEK) and I also notice that he has previously bought three tulip glasses for 17,000 SEK (estimated price 12,000 – 15,000 SEK), 3,000 SEK (estimated price 3,000 – 4,000 SEK) and 11,500 SEK (estimated price 6,000 – 8,000 SEK). Is he a collector? We will never know.

I ask the couple how they feel about selling the glass sculpture and the tulip glass before the auction starts. They have previously told me that feelings for objects have become more important for them as collectors over the years (Ekström 2004). They tell me that they have no feelings for the objects to be sold. It must make it easy to sell, but I wonder if they sometime later in the future will regret selling these items? We will never know.

---

7 I noticed that it was the same buyer, by paying attention to the bidding number mentioned by the auctioneer when closing the bid.

Value(s) created and transformed before and after the auction

The connecting sites between the home and the auction house, before and after the auction, are also of interest when discussing transformation of values. Trajectories are constructed when people bring their items for sale to the auction house, as discussed earlier, but also when they take the purchased items to their homes. A collector I previously interviewed said that when he purchased a glass object, it took some time before he placed the object among the collection: 'I put it out there in the hall and then maybe it will stay there for a week before I move it' (Ekström, 2004). Trajectories are also constructed when collectors move and order their collections at home, for example, rituals related to dusting, cleaning, categorizing and arranging of their little monsters. Belk, Wallendorf and Sherry (1991) discuss that rituals can make objects sacred. Previous interviews with collectors show that the display of their glass objects is carefully considered and varies based on form, color as well as the object's provenience such as designer, glass factory etc. (Ekström, 2005). Collectors sometimes rearrange their glass objects, in particular when new objects are purchased (Ekström, 2005). One family told me that different exhibition themes were arranged in their home (Ekström, 2005). The creativity involved in composition is also something I noticed in previous interviews with collectors, as well as the importance of placing the glass objects in light, in windows or in lightened glass cabinets (Ekström, 2004). In one family, the husband said: 'Glass which is not lit up dies, disappears – you cannot see it' (Ekström, 2004). His wife said that they enjoy turning on the lights that shine on the glass in the evenings: 'Because we did not feel well when there wasn't good lighting' (Ekström, 2004). Previous interviews also indicated that collectors emphasized the importance of regularly cleaning the glass, either by dusting or washing it (Ekström, 2005). A collector explained that she cleans the glass object when coming home from an auction: '... And then when you bring the object home, you wipe it off and wash it and make it nice. Then you can look at it and see if it looks like you thought it would – as it looked when it was at the auction company or wherever it comes from. Of course, it can become a disappointment too' (Ekström, 2004). It was also noticeable that some collectors only dusted their glass, since they were afraid of breaking the glass objects if they washed them (Ekström, 2005).

Finally, it needs to be added that the economic value of glass varies over time. Price changes on glass during the last decades are something glass collectors often mention. Glass collectors I have interviewed earlier have emphasized that they do not see their collections as economical investments. It is the affective value, the joy and curiosity which determine their interest. However, it is my impression that collectors in general seem to be aware of the economic value of their collection. They are continuously exposed to the economic value when seeking for new items, replacing bad copies with good originals, duplicates with unique pieces. Collectors would like to see their collections maintain their value or most preferable, increase in value.

Conclusion

The study focuses on glass, a material which often is perceived as magic. Glass collectors describe its ability to change with light, its color, form and transparency. Transparency which also is related to glass collector's interest in finding the historical value. Collectors both produce and consume value(s). The Actor Network Theory (ANT) has in this chapter been used to illustrate the multidimensional aspects of value and to recognize the creation and transformation of value in a glass auction. ANT makes it possible to understand the relations between value and values and to capture the performative aspects of the auction, the auction being a network of different actors, the people observing, bidding, buying, the personnel at the auction house, the magnificent glass objects for sale, the auction catalogue and the significant bidding paddles.

IV

Monsters Pointing

Fashion and Style in a Commercial and Cultural Borderland

Barbro JOHANSSON

In this chapter fashion and style are discussed in relation to age. When children of 8 – 12 engage in the process of moving from a culturally specified age category – childhood – to another age category – youth – which is defined and apprehended in a rather different way, a lot of diverse actors are set into motion. In the assemblage which might be called teenage-doing, consumer goods are important actors, not in the least clothes and other things that decorate the body, since they make up the performance of the young person, when she/he encounters others.

'Tweens' is a concept referring to children aged around 8 – 12 or those who occupy the space between 'small children' and 'teenagers'. The concept places the individuals in a different context from those referred to as 'pre-adolescents' existing in a 'latent stadium'. The framing of development psychology has here been replaced by a framing much influenced by marketing and economics (Lindstrom, 2003; Sutherland & Thompson, 2003; Quart, 2003). Though the term 'tweens' (alt. 'tweenies') is rather seldom used in everyday Nordic contexts, I will nevertheless take my point of departure in it, since the market connotations associated with it are highly relevant for the data I am going to present and discuss in this text. With tweens a new market segment appears, characterized by their own taste, economic assets as well as influence on the consumption of their families.

To an ethnologist, like myself, the concept is interesting because the use of it says something about children's role in today's society, and because the concept in turn takes part in 'doing' modern childhood in certain ways. The concept fits into a much broader movement, extended far beyond the marketing frame, where children are not only treated as 'becomings' or humans in the making. Today, children are in many ways regarded as 'beings', actively choosing agents here and now. This is the message that is conveyed from quite different parties as childhood researchers, marketers, parents, pedagogues and the Convention on the Rights of the Child. Therefore, it is not the concept 'tweens' as such which is of interest here, but the new ways of relating to children aged 8 – 12, that it reveals, and the possibilities and restraints that follow for the individuals in this age group.

The theoretical perspective I adopt implies that a 'tween' – or whatever one might call a child between 8 and 12 – is not an agent by itself and has no given identity outside the contexts in which its agency – or non-agency – is performed. From a network perspective, agency is considered as an effect of a network, assemblage or hybrid, consisting of humans as well as non-humans, which might be things, texts, narrations, customs, discourses etc., none of them acting or existing separately. 'Translation' is an important concept, when understanding how agency is performed. Ideas move between different contexts through translations, which Latour defines as 'displacement, drift, invention, mediation, creation of a new link that did not exist before and modifies in part the two agents' (Latour, 1993:6). The two agents are the one who translates and the one that is translated. Translation should thus not be mixed up with the linguistic interpretation, where the aim is to reproduce the original meaning as precisely as possible. Instead, translation in a Latourian sense means to place an object, a text or an idea in a new time and a new place (Lindberg 2002:64).

The dichotomy of childhood and youth

The dichotomy of being – becoming has been frequently discussed in childhood research during the last decades (see e.g. Qvortrup, 1987; Alanen, 1992; James, Jenks & Prout, 1998; Lee, 2001; Brembeck, Johansson & Kampmann, 2004; Prout, 2005). It started as a critique of the predominant discourse of development psychology and socialization, and has been used to point out the unequal power relations between adults and children. One important aim has been to stress the ways in which children are reflexive social and cultural beings – active members of society who influence and are influenced by their surroundings. A main objective has been to reveal the power relations between generations and to empower children (Qvortrup, 1994; James & Prout, 1997). Later the concepts have been more and more problematized, e.g. by the fact that 'the human becoming' has turned to represent the common and even desirable modern individual of today (Lee, 2001; Johansson, 2005b; Prout, 2005).

One important aspect of the latter discussions is the recognition of 8 – 12-year-olds as not mainly becoming-adults, but first and foremost becoming-teenagers. In a common understanding of childhood and youth, there are clear differences between a child and a teenager. We have learned that the transition from child to teenager represents a dramatic change – the features ascribed to the teenager highly contrast those ascribed to the child. The cultural dichotomy between childhood and youth tells us that the expected, ideal or normal youth phase is described in terms of identity problems, emotional outbursts, experimenting, revolting against parents and a longing to leave the safe realm of childhood. The corresponding ideal or normal childhood is, on the contrary, focused on the small, safe world, close, lasting relations, harmony and an undramatic, gradual development.

The totally different expectations of these two stages of life, which adjoin each other, must be handled in some way by those who reside there. The space available for those who are 8 – 12 is crisscrossed by ambiguous identity messages, where the young ones, sooner or later, are expected to take a stand and start the complicated process of doing age in a different way than before. In this process material objects are important, not just as symbols, not just as means for the identity work of the young one, but also as co-agents. Make-up, clothes and accessories, as well as the body which they decorate are, just as the individuals, the discourses and the structures, part of doing age and gender. The performance of a teenage boy or a teenage girl implies the participation of active material objects (c.f. Wærdahl, 2003). The concept of 'doing' age and gender stresses that the process is a *practice*. It is by action and by the participation of objects that identities are performed and individuals are placed in age and gender orders (Alanen, 2001; Wærdahl, 2003). Doing age means to relate to an 'other', either to individuals of other ages or to oneself at different stages in life.

I will, in the following discussions, present some cases where boys and girls are constructed as becoming-teenagers and discuss it in connection to the actor network theory. I will investigate the "monsters" consisting of the children's bodies, the clothes, brands, discourses of childhood and youth and the commercial and cultural borderland where these monsters produce, perform and negotiate 'tweenhood' as a matter of age and gender. The data is based on fieldwork carried out among 84 children aged 8 – 12, from two schools in the southwest of Sweden.

Something has happened

Something has happened to me now, 'cause before I didn't care about clothes, I just bought toys. Now it's the opposite. I don't care at all about toys; I never step into a toy store. /.../ Now it's just: "Is there a JC [1] shop here?" If I go into town, then I think... If there's no JC shop there, I don't want to be there.

In the interview, Fredrik, 11, presents a seemingly well thought-out and reflexive image of himself. He describes his great interest in clothes, that his customer loyalty lies with JC and that he spends a lot of time every morning doing his hair and choosing what to wear.

And I'm rather obsessed with hairstyles. If my hair doesn't look good in the morning, I just stand there: "Oh no, this is not good!" And then, I change hairstyles quite often, too. /.../ And then, if I don't find fine clothes. Then I stand there for like five minutes thinking: "No, I can't wear that one today. Not that one either! No!" So I usually choose my clothes in the evening before I go to bed.

In his reflections, Fredrik's concerns about clothes and hairstyle are explicitly related to age, since he refers to a time in life when things were quite different, when toys were the preferred purchase and his taste in clothes was another one.

If I were eight but wore the clothes I am wearing now, I would have hated them. I would never have worn them. I'm pretty sure. /.../ Back then I wore a lot of sloppy clothes, I think. Nerdy. /.../ I used to wear these tracksuit pants (laughs).

The way 'the becoming-teenager Fredrik' is constructed in this interview can be understood in terms of performance. One important aspect of viewing actions as performances is that it is not an individual with a given identity who acts, but identity is constructed within the performative process (Butler, 1993; Petersson, 2003; Mörck and Tullberg, 2004). With the concept of performance the idea that individuals and groups have identities, which they express in clothes and hairstyle, is contrasted with a view of fashion as a main aspect in the construction of identity, a process of change, ambiguities and conflicts (Mörck and Tullberg, 2004:4f). The above examples show some crucial elements or 'actants' (Latour 1999, Callon 1999) in the performative process of the assemblage doing 'Fredrik'. In his translation of tweenhood, Fredrik arranges these elements in a somewhat dichotomist pattern, comparable with the dichotomy of child – teenager: His old tracksuit pants are contrasted with his new clothes from JC, the toy store with the JC store and the constant changes in hairstyle with a memory of childhood when appearance was not one of Fredrik's concerns. 'Age does not just tell what one is, but also what one will become and what one has been', sociologist Ivar Frønes writes (1995:190).

[1] JC, Jeans & Clothes, is a major Swedish fashion retailer.

Age can be regarded as a 'social strategy' (ibid.), where identity is a process following a certain trajectory (Wærdahl, 2003:215). The individual looks at himself/herself in the light of the past and the expected future. Fredrik describes how he has left one phase of life and is now on his way somewhere else – to become a teenager. As the interview continued it turned out that the translation process involves, not only Fredrik's body and its decorations, but also his friends in school. Fredrik is interviewed together with his best friend Harry.

Fredrik: I think it's nice if I have really good-looking clothes and I'm really satisfied with them, then it's so awfully good to wear them.

Barbro: *Mm. What? How does it feel?*

Fredrik: Well, it sort of, just... I can feel like... If I buy new clothes, that I'm really proud of, then I look forward to going to school the next day and wearing them.

Harry: Yes, 'cause then friends always come up and say: "Did you buy new clothes? Oh, how nice!"

Fredrik: Yes, Fanny usually says so. If I buy new clothes, she always says so: "Oh, your new clothes are so nice!"

Anthropologists Alison Clarke and Daniel Miller challenge the post-modern view of consumers playfully and undauntedly choosing among styles and identities. They claim that anxiety is a main aspect of people's relation to fashion (Clarke and Miller, 2002). When we choose our clothes it is out of the anxiety of not fitting in and of being distinguished from others in an uncomfortable way. The truth is that we do not really know what we like; it depends on how our outfit functions in relation to others (ibid.). Clarke and Miller associate this with a long-lasting theoretical discussion on the contradictory desires for social imitation and individual differentiation (Simmel, 1971; Entwistle, 2000). Simmel claims that the problem arises with modern society, where people meet for short moments, with no other possibility of judging each other than by the appearance, and where one is always at risk of being the object of the (critical) gaze of others (Simmel, 1971; Lee, 2001). With modernity, new possibilities for the creation of identity arose, Entwistle (2000) claims. 'It unfixed individuals from traditional communities, placing them in the 'melting-pot' of the city, and it extended the commodities available for purchase to an ever widening circle of people' (ibid.:117).

The dilemma is obvious in my study. Both girls and boys are very concerned with how to be equal but not identical, how to fit in without copying. Shopping as an important common activity is one expression of the phenomenon. It is crucial to get a confirmation from others that one's choice of clothes and hairstyle etc. is okay. Fredrik's story about the agony in front of the mirror in the mornings is a good illustration of the predicament, and so is the encounter on the schoolyard with his fashion-conscious friends and their opinions.

It is also worth noticing that a specific kind of 'boyishness' is constructed in the 'monster' Fredrik. It is a gender performance, which is quite different from those of most other boys at his school, who have more typical boyish interests such as computers, sports and motorbikes. As the quotation above hints, it is mainly the girls who respond to his fashion consciousness and his concern about appearance. One could say that Fredrik makes a gender anti-program (see Hansson, this volume), when performing a less common male subjectivity. Even the fashion interest of Fredrik's best friend Harry seems to be mostly theoretical; he admits that he, though having his wardrobe full of clothes, usually wears a few favorites, and that his main interest is to drive his motorbike. Still, though, clothes and fashion seem to be part of the cement that hold the two boys together, Fredrik being the one who expresses it, and Harry having the role as supporting company.

A mutual construction

But there is more to say about the assemblage in which the agency of 'becoming-teenager Fredrik' is performed. The fashion company JC is repeatedly mentioned in the interview with Fredrik and Harry. JC is the self-evident target of their shopping trips, in the store the boys get information on the latest fashion and inspiration for purchases and in the schoolyard the clothes are displayed and judged by peers. Without a doubt, JC is an influent actor in the construction of mainly Fredrik's 'becoming-teenager-subjectivity'. But it is not just a one-way process; the boys in their turn construct JC.

Regarding subjectivity as an assemblage means that it is possible for an individual to appear in several ways, none of them being more authentic than the others. Subjectivity is created through different elements functioning as 'prostheses' (Haraway 1991), or 'extensions' (Lee 2001). Extensions creating the assemblage 'Fredrik' are for instance his new shirt, the hair-styling gel, his classmates and the company JC. When JC becomes part of the assemblage it also becomes the target of reconstruction. There are no inherent characteristics that distinguish a macro-actor like a company from a micro-actor like an individual or an object. According to Bruno Latour and Judith Butler there are no given, stable structures, neither states and companies nor patriarchy and market economy, which people either have to conform to or revolt against. What is conceived as continuity, as the power of the structure upon individuals, is instead the result of ongoing ‘repetitions’ or ‘translations’. Political and economic systems, institutions and ideologies exist only by constantly being made anew in everyday practice.

But at the same time every performance is new, every repetition or translation unique, and therefore each one also implies a potential treachery. This is the dilemma of the power, Latour states; to be able to grow the power must be delegated, but as soon as this is done, the total control of the process gets lost (Latour, 1998). The companies who sell products to children and youths are painfully conscious of how uncontrollable their market is. The positive image of a company is only maintained as long as the customers continue to establish it. In the literature aimed at marketers, young consumers stand out as knowing and demanding; they know what they want and they can passionately hold on to a brand, but at the same time they are unpredictable and notoriously unfaithful (Lindstrom, 2003; Sutherland and Thompson, 2003).

Fredrik and Harry are mainly faithful JC customers. Their translations of JC are based on their loyalty, and here moral aspects are added to the assemblage. For example, the boys claim that a certain detail on a garment from JC was found in a distorted shape on a garment from another fashion company, thereby suggesting that JC represents the authentic, while other companies plagiarize. The boys also think that JC advertises less than other fashion companies, that they are more restricted and serious in their marketing. This is in line with Fredrik and Harry’s opinion – that there is too much advertising on television, and their opinions, in turn, are part of an advertising-restrained discourse, even present in some companies’ rhetoric. From their description, JC is a company, which they can identify themselves with, even when it comes to marketing. Thereby JC and the boys use and construct each other in a mutual process.

The hybrid ‘girl-thongs’

Barbro: *Then there has been a discussion about thongs. Some people think that ”Well, but thongs are so nice” and others think, “No, you don’t have to wear them”, and…*

Anna-Clara, 11: No, you shouldn’t wear them.

Sanna, 11 (laughs): No.

Anna-Clara: Not at our age. Or, if one is of our age, then I really don't think one should wear them.

Sanna: We're still too small.

Anna-Clara: Yes, I think it's... Frankly it's ridiculous to wear them at our age.

Barbro: *When do you think one should start wearing them?*

Sanna: Maybe at the beginning of junior high school or something like that?

Anna-Clara: Yes. 8th or 9th grade.

Sanna: 7th, 8th grade, I think.

Anna-Clara: 8th, 9th grade. That's when girls start to be mature enough for it.

Barbro: *Why do you have to be mature to wear thongs?*

Anna-Clara: But it looks so ridiculous, like...

Sanna: Yes.

Anna-Clara: ...when you are, like, in the 5th grade, it looks ridiculous to you walk around with thongs.

Sanna (laughs): Yes.

The hybrid character of actors implies that 'girl', 'thongs' and 'girl-thongs' are to be conceived of as three different actors or assemblages. It is the third of these actors that is related to above. As the quotation shows, this actor (monster, hybrid, assemblage) apart from a girl's body and a garment also includes social relations between girls and discourses of 'age' and 'maturity'. When trying to understand the 'girl-thongs' it is necessary to avoid ascribing essences to the 'girl' and the 'thongs', but, as sociologist Mike Michael states, to see the new associations, goals and translations which the new hybrid entails (Michael, 2000:26). He quotes Latour: 'Neither the subject nor the object, nor their goals are fixed forever. We have to shift our attention to this unknown X, this hybrid which can truly be said to act' (ibid.). In his book *Reconnecting culture, technology and nature,* Michael analyzes some common Western hybrids: walking boots, road rage, the couch potato and the 'hudogledog' (human + doglead + dog). In the following sections, I will investigate the hybrid/monster 'girl-thongs'.

In the conversation, the thongs are placed within an assemblage where bodies of different ages and maturity are central elements, and so is the critical gaze, which judges the imagined performances of thongs and body. There is a short negotiation between the girls concerning at what age a body is mature enough to be dressed in thongs (13 – 14 or 14 – 15), showing that the space where childhood and youth meet is intersected by a lot of very concrete categorizations and drawing of borderlines. Together, the girls create a difference between those who seem 'ridiculous', by wearing thongs, though they are only 11 years old, and themselves, who understand that one is not mature enough for such a garment before the age of 14 or 15. Two dichotomies are present: the one between 'thongs for youth' and 'girls' briefs for 11-year-olds' and the one between 'ridiculous 11-year-olds dressed in thongs' and 'sensible 11-year-olds dressed in accordance with their level of maturity'. The thongs are judged as a garment for those who are mature, at the same time as girls who wear common briefs appear as the most sensible and mature. Dressing in a way, which has no correspondence to maturity of the body, becomes here a sign of immaturity.

To develop the discussion further it might be useful to draw upon the concept of '11-year-ness' (Wenzer, 2002). 11-year-ness (just as 10-year-ness, 14-year-ness etc.) is the place assigned to individuals at a certain age, a place with its own history, conveying ideas about what, in this case, an 11-year-old 'is' or 'should be'. At the same time 11-year-ness functions as a category of subjectivity production, in the processes where 11-year-ness and the 11-year-old individuals mutually construct each other (ibid, p. 15f). An 11-year-old has a certain range of available subjectivities. The 11-year-old girl which Anna-Clara and Sanna relate to has not yet reached puberty and is consequently not physically mature to dress in a garment associated with adulthood and sexuality. However, this does not prevent the girls to live up to their 11-year-ness in a sensible way, by refraining from wearing garments, which are not 'suitable' for an 11-year-old. One might say that the girls are constructed as 11-year-old 'beings', while girls of equal age wearing thongs are constructed as ridiculous 'teenager-becomings'.

Anna-Clara's and Sanna's critique against 11-year-olds wearing thongs is a critique against insufficient consistency. Their 11-year-ness is no ambiguous place, where a child's body is combined with an adult's garment. 11-year-ness receives its value and strength in being coherent and logic. At the same time the fact is that many girls of 11 – 12 reach their puberty and develop a body on which the thongs 'fit'. Clear borders between proper and improper might be more difficult to keep up with for the girls, than what they appear to be in this interview. We should also remember that the interview as a specific genre is a powerful truth-producing actor, which assigns certain subjectivities to the interviewees.

Body and sexuality

In the discussion between Anna-Clara, Sanna and me, certain elements of 'girl-thongs' are brought to the fore, such as age, body, maturity and sensibility. But present in the situation, though not explicitly articulated is also for example the connection to sexuality. In public debates such as articles and letters-to-the-editor in newspapers and magazines or discussion forums on the Internet, a recurring issue is the connection between clothes and sexuality, the ways in which clothes, carrying different sexual connotations, are marketed for and worn by children (c.f. Johansson, 2005a). The arguments in these debates are that the girls, wearing clothes that expose the body in certain ways, become objects of a sexualized male gaze. The discourse of the male gaze implies that the man's desire is directed towards the woman and the woman's desire is to arouse the man's desire, something she accomplishes by manipulating her body in different ways (Mulvey, 1989; Hirdman, 2001).

In the translation process the meanings and the agency of an object, such as the thongs, differ depending on by whom and in which context it is translated. Discourses of sexuality and of the male gaze are possible, but not compulsory actants in the translation. Girls of 11 can e.g. dress in thongs just because they think it is nice-looking. The argument here is that thongs are the most appropriate choice, when one wears light or tight pants, because then the edge of the briefs is not visible. But when the discourse of the male gaze is prevalent in the hybrid 'girl-thongs', it transforms the whole assemblage in certain ways. For Anna-Clara, the aesthetical aspect then comes into conflict with aspects of maturity and sexuality.

Barbro: Those who wear thongs, they say it's so ugly when the edge of the briefs is visible, when you wear such pants.

Anna-Clara: Mm. That's an advantage, but. Sort of, if you wear tight pants, that's when you should wear thongs, but it's also then one can see that you wear them. /.../ 'Cause, I think it's much more embarrassing to wear them, when you can tell that you are wearing them. /.../

Barbro: Sure. If there are no visible panty lines, then it's obvious that you are wearing thongs.

Anna-Clara: Yes.

The aesthetical advantage is here countered by a revelation of an inconsistent acting of 11-year-ness. If Anna-Clara gives in to the wish of dressing nicely, she would, at the same time, demonstrate that she has dressed above her 'level of maturity'. What is most visible here, is that which is not visible – the embarrassing thongs. And in the imagined performance referred to in the interview, the thongs take part in revealing that nothing more than the pants' fabric covers the girl's buttocks. They show a smooth surface, which might give associations to naked skin and thereby pave the way for sexual interpretations, which Anna-Clara is probably not comfortable with (cf. Berggren Torell, 2004).

Being a trendsetter

However, the 'girl-thongs' is a monster with many possible appearances. As stated, being 8 – 12 years old means being aware that one sooner or later has to deal with how to solve the problem of becoming a teenager. One might, as some of the girls in the above examples, choose, what sociologist Randi Wærdahl calls, 'delayed anticipation', postponing the concerns of youth some years (Wærdahl, 2003:217ff). Other children in the study have instead taken on the strategy of 'explored anticipation' of their forthcoming teenagehood (ibid.). Fredrik above presented one example of this strategy. He constructed a clear break between 'before' and 'now', between a time when he was nerdy and today when he is cool. It is also possible to go through the process in a more continuous way, where the element which holds different ages and stages together might be precisely such a thing as 'coolness'. This is a strategy, which seems to be applicable to three 12-year-old girls, Emma, Louise and Gabriella. In the interview I ask them if they use thongs.

Emma: Yes, sometimes. At discos and such.

Louise: But not so often.

Gabriella. No, not now. Before.

Louise: When we thought it was cool to wear it.

Barbro: *I see. So it's not as cool now?*

Louise: Yes, it was, when we were younger or kind of /…/ In 4th or 5th grade. Then we thought it was cool 'cause nobody else wore it.

Gabriella. Yes, 'cause now everybody is wearing them. But back then, only a few were wearing them. Then it was cool.

The concerns for Emma, Louise and Gabriella are not about what thongs might signify of age or maturity. The garment is not placed in an assemblage involving developmental discourse, where there exists a certain point of time when the thongs fit on a girl's body. The value of the garment does not lie in the way it distinguishes different life stages from each other, but in the way it distinguishes clothes that everybody wears from clothes that only those who are cool wear. Neither do the girls explicitly associate the thongs to sexuality. This way of framing deprives the thongs of the essential character they had in for instance Anna Clara's and Sanna's rhetoric. For them, thongs in themselves represented adulthood/youth, maturity and possibly also sexuality. As Louise and her friends talk about it, the character of the thongs is entirely dependent on the context. They only have value when taking part in a performance where they are rare. If everybody wears them, they are no more or less worth than any other underwear. The task for the girls in this example seems not so much to deal with how to solve their 12-year-ness, but rather with how to stay cool, regardless of age. Staying cool means being in the forefront, that is constantly moving one's positions forward, hereby of course sometimes connecting to symbols associated with sexuality, which is a frequently used actant in the performance of teenagehood. Another example they give is that all three girls have several holes in their ears. They were the only ones who had them before, but 'now sort of everybody in the class wants to do it', and that's when it starts to get boring instead. Now tattoos are appealing instead, and Louise says that she can see herself at least getting a henna tattoo. The focal point is thus neither age, maturity, consistency nor sexuality, though each of them could be drawn into the 'coolness assemblage'.

Normative or subversive

As ethnologist Magdalena Peterson suggests in her doctoral thesis (2003) performance can be understood both as normative and as subversive (ibid., Butler, 1990; MacKenzie, 2001). Social life is constantly organized in normative ways, where the individual is presented with expectations of how to appear and behave. But the possibility of 'treachery' (Latour, 1998) and subversion is always present in the translation processes, and it might be that an anti-program is performed.

In literature critical to consumption, agency is located outside the individual, at the companies and marketers, who persuade and seduce, while the young consumers are given the victims' role. The title of journalist Alissa Quart's book, *Branded* (2003), stresses that it is not only the case that brands are more important, but that young people themselves act as brands. Young people often wish to act for a good cause, Quart argues, but instead of giving energy to for instance non-profit organization, the brand is what they struggle for. It is the brand, which they show loyalty to and it is the message of the brand, which they propagate for (ibid.). Quart, who takes her point of departure in U.S. conditions, claims that young people's self-images and values have been distorted by the 'commercial frenzy surrounding them' (ibid.:17). Sociologist Juliet B. Schor represents the same view in her book *Born to buy* (2004), where she criticizes American companies who pay to get direct access to children and youth in school by sponsoring, advertising and supplying textbooks. What used to be sacred temples of learning now have more in common with the mall, Schor declares (ibid.)

However, two British researchers, sociologist Rachel Russell and business administrator Melissa Tyler (2004), assert that 'branding', what the companies do to the young people, is countered by 'bricolage', what the young people do to the companies and their symbols. In this process the youths make the symbols to their own by re-definitions and recreation (ibid.:4). Russell and Tyler (2004) have studied British girls during some years in their transition from childhood to youth. They show that the construction of the girls as teenagers is a supremely social activity, where the girls, the shopping environments and the commodities they buy as well as other commodities that are for sale, are important actors. Belongings do not only take part in creating teenage identity, but also function as a glue in the group of girls, for example in that the girls own similar things or share the same taste or shopping experiences. Expressed in actor network terms it presents an example of how a process, where certain actants are involved, can be translated in quite different ways, depending on who is given the role as an actor. Not only can the company or the individual be actors, but also the brand, the clothes, the bodies, the group dynamic and critical texts, such as those of Quart and Schor. 'The intermixing of the human and non-human is intrinsic to human society', Michael (2000:21) writes.

Louise, Gabriella and Emma gave an example of a bricolage process, where different objects and appearances took part in performing 'coolness'. But there are other ways of relating to appearance and fashion, which might be more problematic to the companies. In the interviews I asked the children why they put on just the clothes they wore that day. Many of them gave answers like these:

I just put on something. Something my parents pick out. (Boy, 8)

The clothes I can put on the quickest. (Boy, 10)

I didn't think so much. Mom usually picks out the clothes (Girl, 10)

Well I don't bother much... It's not anything special (Boy, 10).

In contrast to for example Fredrik, some of the children seem to care very little about their clothes, having the only demand that the clothes should be comfortable and the right size. That is however not the same as saying that they would go to school wearing any clothes. Most of them could give examples of clothes that they would not wear at school, for instance clothes which were too dressy or too ordinary. I got the impression that the possibility to ignore clothes and fashion paradoxically enough was dependent on the competence of dressing in a way which neither stood out positively nor negatively. Sabrina, 8, says that when one is older one wants to be cool and nice-looking, but at her age one 'wants to be ordinary'. And to be ordinary is, as I understand her, both to dress as most others do, and not to care so much about fashion and style. 'Fashion, as a collective translation process, also functions as a release from the responsibility of individual choice', Czarniawska and Joerges (1996) argue.

In marketing literature tweens and youths are portrayed as fashion and brand conscious, and the concerns of the companies are to compete with each other and make one's own brand stand out as the most attractive. But the problem with children with no interest in fashion seems to be less addressed. Especially interviews with many boys were characterized by me indefatigably asking questions about taste and style choices, while the answers remained politely choppy. Nisse, 11, wore pants, which his mother bought for him once. He had had his sweater for several years and did not remember where it came from. His friend Olle wore a sweater, which his sister gave him. In different ways I tried to find out the fashion rules at school.

Barbro: *Has anyone ever been teased, or have you ever commented on someone's clothes?*

Nisse: I don't know. Not in our class.

Olle: No, I don't think so. I usually play bandy during the breaks, so I don't know anything about that.

Barbro: *Don't you usually talk to each other about clothes and such things?*

Olle: No.

Barbro: *If something is nice-looking, do you usually comment on that?*

Both: Yes.

Barbro: *Which clothes are nice-looking?*

Nisse: I don't know.

Olle: Well, all clothes are nice in some way.

Barbro: *Perhaps fashion is not that important to you?*

Both: No.

Nisse: It's so tiresome.

Barbro: *Is it tiresome?*

Nisse: I never look in fashion magazines and those kinds of things. I don't follow fashion.

The adornments of the body are not active elements in Nisse's and Olle's subjectivity productions. Other children at their school tell me that there are discussions about people's choice of clothing, but these two boys haven't noticed that. Fashion is not only uninteresting, it is tiresome, they state. If one's mom or big sister takes the responsibility of purchasing the clothes, then one does not have to take energy from playing bandy or other more interesting activities. When Nisse tells me that he does not follow fashion it is thus not a regret of insufficient competence, but rather a declaration, where he says that he prioritizes different things in life. He is not interested in fashion and he does not want to be either. Gender is also performed in the interview; to be unconcerned about clothes and fashion is a common masculine subjectivity. When style and fashion lack an identity creating function, other values can emerge. Common benevolent equality thinking can be noticed in Olle's assertion that all clothes are nice in some way.

Olle's and Nisse's attitudes on clothes can be regarded as subversive and as an anti-program related to the program of fashion-conscious tweens. This anti-program might become a threat to the capitalistic market economy, which is dependent on a never-ending purchase desire of the consumers. In the (dream) world of the marketers, children are constantly connected, curious of the latest trends, ready to immediately join in and bring their peers with them. Martin Lindstrom enthusiastically expresses this view in his book *Brandchild:*

> The instant communication across the globe between tweens has made it possible for the entire generation to adopt and develop certain trends and keep them alive for months. I call this phenomenon *fish streaming*. In theory, one tween can influence tens of others, and in almost no time at all millions of tweens are following (Lindstrom 2003:5).

The children who Lindstrom refers to here are not the ones who use the same favorite sweater one year after another, who are uninterested in fashion, never read fashion magazines and who think that all clothes are nice in some way. Translation is not neutral, it is an act of power. What marketers like Lindstrom do, is translate the will and the quality of 'the tween' into one single character, thereby creating their own ideal customer. The children themselves do their own translations or bricolage, affected by the companies but still deeply uncontrollable by them, thereby constituting endless sales possibilities as well as serious threats to the survival of the companies. The possible subversion of children lies for example in *not* giving attention to fashion and trends. In the extension their attitudes can be linked to the consumption critical movement, thereby being part of a powerful global assemblage.

Performing tweenhood

The focus of this chapter has been on the role of fashion and style for the ages between 8 and 12, when 'tweens' are engaged in a process of becoming-teenager. Influential theories of development psychology, pediatrics and pedagogy have arranged our understanding of childhood and youth in accordance with psychological and biological criteria. Ideals of childhood as protected, carefree and undramatic are just as established as expectations of the teenage years as being characterized by change, revolt and breaking up. This makes the ages before 13 a time of anticipation and experimentation of identity.

In the discussion about typical teenage or adult clothes, the children could distance themselves from the teenage ideal in favor of a consistent '11-year-ness' where one is 'a child' until the body (and perhaps also the character) shows something else. The dichotomy of 'being – becoming' is actualized here. As these girls put it, it is obvious that one can be a 'being' implying that one lives up to the expectations of a person of certain age, to be a typical or normal 11-year-old. In the girls' stories consistency is an important sign of the individual residing on 'the stair landing of 11-year-ness', another sign is that one does not aspire to belong to a higher 'developmental stage', but being satisfied with being exactly where one is.

Another way of doing tweenhood is taking the point of departure, not in age and maturity, but in the social context, where such a thing as 'coolness' becomes a vital actor, which incorporates social relations, clothes, styles, artifacts and body in its assemblage. Sexuality might or might not play a prominent part in the coolness monster, depending on how the specific event is framed.

The study moreover has shown examples of how to be a becoming-teenager without putting any efforts on clothes and fashion. Such an attitude might be conceived as a threat against the fashion industry, which is dependent on constant renewal. Maybe that is so, maybe the conduct of these children is subversive, an undermining movement which drains the commercial messages of their reliability and influence. Or maybe the constant desire for new stuff is simply more than just about clothes. Being a boy of 12 and owning a motorbike, which one is not allowed to drive before 16, is just as an effective way to do both gender and age. Besides, it is a documented fact that market economy is able to enroll all possible variations of consumption to its network, even the resistance (Slater, 1997).

Being a tween is however not necessarily the same as being a becoming-teenager. Children of 8 – 12 are, just as individuals of all other ages, sometimes beings and sometimes becomings. In this chapter I have given examples of different ways of performing tweenhood and the crucial influence of actants other than the child, such as artifacts, clothes, discourses, brands and companies. In the interviews the children in the study presented different ways of relating to artifacts, thereby also presenting different ways of performing age and gender. By taking a standpoint where agency is not essentially situated in a certain actor, it is possible to see the displacements and reinterpretations going on, and also that there is an in-built uncertainty concerning the continuation of the process. No actor has full control over what happens, but everybody tries to get it. Companies, clothes, brands and individuals belong to assemblages, where they mutually construct each other.

Every actor does something, but the choices are not free and every actor tries to support his/her/its significance as best as it can be done. The individuals choose or drop, combine goods in unique ways, transform and reload commodities, which they make their belongings. The corporations keep informed of psychological theories and make qualitative studies with focus groups and interviews, and establish personal relations and loyalties in order to influence consumers. The clothes display the body in certain ways, for instance by concealing or revealing different body parts. They affect the conduct of the individual, for example by admitting more or less freedom of movement or by occupying the individual's time when she/he is shopping or choosing what to wear. The clothes also do something to the observer, catching his/her eyes and arousing desire or antipathy, for the clothes as well as the one who wears them. All of these multifaceted processes make up the cultural and commercial borderland where the tweenhood monster is constructed in the context of fashion and style.

A Tale of a Car Sharing Organization (CSO) Monster

Pernilla JONSSON

> Certainly the thought of owning a car is appealing! Go wherever you want, when you want to. But this dream of freedom crashes when you encounter the reality of traffic jams, environmental consequences and a strained private economy. Both the public transportation system and private car ownership have its advantages. A shared car is a way to use the advantages and minimize the downsides of owning a car. (...) In our car sharing organization we share the workload. The car sharing organization has no employees, as our members share occurring tasks to keep the costs down. As a member you'll have to put in 2 – 5 hours a month. Examples of workgroups are car-care, purchasing, insurance, information, IT, member service and education.(...).[1]

This quote is taken from the homepage of Majorna's car sharing organization (CSO). By becoming a member of a CSO, a consumer gains access to the CSO fleet of cars, thereby he or she may book a car when in need to drive somewhere instead of actually having to own one. CSO's were first started in the late 1980's, mainly in European countries such as Switzerland, Germany and Sweden (Sperling and Shaheen, 1999). Internationally there are many kinds of CSO's; some are very small with only one car owned by a few neighboring enthusiasts, some are larger but still employ the cooperative ownership form, while others are commercial enterprises. The largest CSO in Europe, Mobility in Switzerland has over 60,000 members[2]. In 2004, the largest CSO in Sweden was Majorna's car sharing, still a cooperative owned by its more than 300 members sharing 29 cars[3].

From a consumer point of view, the advantages of the car sharing organizations are often described as considerable. As the fixed costs of the cars are shared between the members, it's much cheaper to be a member of a CSO than to privately own a car, provided that the consumer drives less than 20,000 km/year (Jakobsson, 2002). In polls, conducted by human ecologist Dr. Meritt Polk, 90% of the members of Majorna's car sharing agree that they joined to get cheap access to a car (Polk, 2000). Apart from the fact that a privately owned car often requires a large financial commitment for the individual consumer, it might also bring unforeseen costs, like repairs etc. Therefore, the

[1] 2004 – 09 – 22: www.majornas-bilkoop.se/default2.asp, author's translation

[2] Mobility Annual report 2004

[3] 2004 – 09 – 22: www.majornas-bilkoop.se/default2.asp

costs are more predictable for the individual consumer. Moreover, as the main expense of car sharing occurs when consumers reserve and use the car, they can regulate how much they spend every month.

Besides the financial benefits of car sharing, it has been reported that the main reasons for joining a CSO is the experienced convenience of car sharing (Polk, 2000; Jakobsson, 2002; Sperling and Shaheen, 1999). For example, when driving a car sharing car the members do not have to search for a parking space or worry about parking tickets as the vehicles have assigned parking spaces. As taking care of the car is a collective responsibility in a CSO, many car sharers feel that the amount of time they spend on the CSO is less than when owning a car privately (Polk, 2000).

The process behind booking and using a car works as follows [4]: When in need of a car, the car sharer books a car over the Internet or by phone using a smartcard as his/her identification. The card is downloaded with the booking information and when the car sharer picks up the car, the card is placed on the windshield of the car and the car opens. Thus, the individual smartcard works as a key to the car. The smartcard is then plugged into a card reader inside the car, which registers the amount of fuel used, the mileage traveled etc. This information is then used to bill the car sharer through an IT system. The car sharer leaves the car in an assigned parking space and is later billed for the trip. With this type of process, the system functions rather smoothly and the administrative costs of sharing cars are quite low, at least when compared to sharing cars with no such coordinating information system.

If applying ANT to car sharing, a CSO may be seen as consisting of human and non-human actants connected through the actions members perform. These actions are regulated through how the members have created agreed-upon understandings concerning car sharing. For example a person has to do certain things in order to become a member, the cars are supposed to be used in certain ways etc. Thus, one may see the CSO as the result of institutionalized actions which folds along similar patterns and time rhythms in everyday life. For example, to book a car one may surf to the Majorna homepage on the Internet, where one clicks around to find an available car and then goes through a certain procedure to book it. Other such regulations are found around the work-groups; members have to perform their duties with certain regularities etc. The CSO really consists of all the items and actions associated with its existence. The repetition of CSO related actions, involving material objects assigned to the organization, like booking a car is really what upholds this monster into

4 Ibid

what we perceive as a CSO in everyday life. It seems like the CSO may be seen as a phenomenon with all the necessary ingredients to qualify as some kind of interesting monster of which a tale may be told.

This chapter is based on material gathered for my doctoral thesis *Capturing the elusive simplifier*. In this chapter I have chosen to use material concerning car sharing organizations in general and Majorna car sharing organization in particular. The material includes in-depth interviews with 14 informants from the Majornas CSO. It also includes the results of a variety of research reports on car sharing and participant observation at a car sharing conference in Stockholm 2002. In addition I had an expert interview with Per Schillander, who works with car sharing for the Swedish road administration. In this chapter, I have taken this material and reflected upon it with inspiration from Latour but also some theory from consumer research. The aim of the chapter is to analyze the CSO monster, how it came to be, and what it may tell us about the world.

A Latourian monster is characterized by how it changes with the connections it makes to actants. The connections and the actants all change with time; some connections are stronger, others quite easily lose their attachment to the monster, while others must be ripped from the monster with some force. The interesting thing about monsters to me is that they seem to be living creatures with an unpredictable nature. In order to understand the CSO monster we need to start to understand it in a context of consumer society.

A CSO monster emerges

In consumer research theory, consumption is described as being about expressing, communicating, displaying individual and social identity (Douglas and Isherwood, 1979; Belk, 1988; Richins, 1994 etc.), being a member of a car sharing organization should also say something about who you are on a culturally significant or symbolic level. When I asked the informants why they became members of the CSO, the vast majority of them concurred with the notions found also in other CSO studies. They saw the organization as a way to gain access to a car without having to assume the financial responsibilities of owning one. This seems like an obvious and straightforward explanation. However it doesn't say much about the symbolic significance of a CSO. Holt (1997) argues that collective understandings of the symbolic meaning of how a consumption item is used in a consumer group emerge from relational differences to other collective interpretations of symbolic value. Therefore understanding how car sharers view the privately owned car is essential in understanding the symbolic value of car sharing. Below, a male car sharer illustrates his view on the symbolic value of cars:

> The car has been defined as private property by the car industry; you gain your identity through your car, which is a very strange idea indeed. Cars should be a means of transportation. But as one of the design managers at Volvo said: It took us a while to realize that we are in the fashion industry. And that's exactly what the car is today. And that is why we have the fast depreciation of (new) cars, the large sales volumes of new cars and the environmental damages induced by cars. Right now, really huge, stunning cars with four-wheel drive are really trendy. The SUV[5]'s, I mean, with lots of engine power and so on. And that's totally crazy! (M, early 40s, CS)

The quote can be said to display this kind of a relational difference in interpretation described by Holt (1997). This car sharer maintains that the car industry has transformed the car from a mean of transportation into a fashion item, something this car sharer strongly opposes. He emphasizes the use-value of cars rather than their supposed symbolic value as fashion objects. After having analyzed most of the other interviews it seemed to me that most of the people I interviewed, would concur with the view that car sharing is a way to reinstate the utility value of the car. Most informants in this study describe status consumption in general as something useless and into which people are duped by the alluring surfaces of advertising and other marketing tactics. Most of the interviewed car sharers opposed strongly against people building their identities through consumption. Consumers who buy brand name goods just in order to look nice are fooled, as the informants explained the phenomena to me.

For example one female car sharer explained that she believes that it is the pressure from consumer society, which forces consumers to consume. She said that this pressure from consumer society makes people need certain things – like a brand name car – in order to 'fit into' the societal norm. This informant described that by not owning a car and instead being a member of a CSO, a person could be seen as having an alternative to create an identity to that of owning a brand name car. Kozinets (2002) describes how consumers perform emancipatory practices in order to distance the consumers from the market. It seems that car sharing may be seen as an example of an emancipatory practice, as it helps car sharers express an identity untainted by commercial meanings inscribed in brand name cars. Car sharing may thus be viewed as something

5 SUV, sports utility vehicle, usually used to refer to four-wheel drive city jeeps like Volvo XC90, Landrover, Range rover, Mitsubishi Pajero etc.

more than just an easy way to get access to a car. It can be seen as making a statement 'against' creating identity through consumption.

Historically, widespread car usage has grown at the same pace as the emergence of consumer society, at least in the western world. Celebrated in ads and commercials the car can be said to be one of the most forceful symbols of consumer society. In the green movement[6], on the other hand, the car has somewhat become a symbol for the downsides of consumer society (Ottosson and Ottosson, 1998). From the green movement, widespread car usage has been heavily criticized due to a wide range of issues from the most obvious; polluting the environment, but also for transforming the townscape, enhancing stress and irritation in everyday life and even contributing to isolation in society (Ottosson and Ottosson, 1998). Every attempt from the green movement to persuade people to use cars less and bikes more has failed miserably, and private car ownership/usage is still the predominant way to organize private transportation in consumer society. Car sharing has often been mentioned as part of a "greener" way to consume private transportation (Ottosson and Ottoson, 1998; Lundgren, 1999; Rhodin, 2001; Jakobsson, 2002). Given the background of CSO's as emerging from green ideology, they may be seen as born to be 'little green monsters' embodying critique towards consumer society. Thereby our CSO monster has gained color, and a direction; it is a little green monster embodying a yearning for a different society.

Our CSO monster begins to take form. It does not just consist of the human and non-human actors connected to each other by actions. The members seem to inscribe certain meanings and values to the CSO. As the CSO emerges as an alternative to how a car is 'defined by the car industry', it may be regarded as a rebellious act aiming to change the way we use cars in consumer society. Therefore it may be seen as an 'anti-program' (see also Hansson in this volume) fighting the dominant 'program' of the 'car' concept and how it is black-boxed as privately owned[7] in consumer society. Thus, we have a monster at war, against the car industry. By adding connections and enrolling more

6 By the green movement I refer to what Castells (1997) refers to as a global network or heterogeneous organizations united by a common aim; to save the environment from destruction.

7 I am aware that leasing, renting, having a company car and so on are alternative forms to car ownership in our society, however, in spite of the many forms of financing a car, the general idea is that a car should be somehow assigned to an individual or a household unit. Therefore I have chosen to ignore the multiple other ways one may use to access a car, as these all are united by this general underlying idea of tying the car to one or two users rather than to a collective of users as in the case of the CSO's.

cars and consumers into its network, its activities may be seen as a guerilla like rebellion challenging the dominant way of using cars in consumer society.

The weapons and tactics of a little green monster at war

As a little green monster aiming to change the world, the CSO may be described as offering an alternative that is fundamentally different from the privately owned car. However, the difference is not inherent in the visual surface of the product, a car sharing car is not fundamentally different than a privately owned car at least not at a first glance.

When examining the fleet of cars owned by CSO, one discovers that it often consists of non-premium brands like Opel, Toyota, Ford and smart cars [8]. This is also true for the car fleet at Majorna's CSO. The pride of the Majorna car fleet is the Toyota Prius which is an environmentally friendly hybrid engine car. This seems to comply well with the CSO monster. Still the cars used in the CSO are of global brands. In companies such as Toyota, Opel and Ford marketers and advertisers work continuously in trying to attach symbolic values to car brands. Opel, for instance, market themselves with the slogan 'fresh thinking – better cars' [9]. Toyota, as it seems, tries to attach a whole philosophy to their brand with 'the Toyota way' [10] and Ford's slogan is 'feel the difference'. Although the aim of brand tactics such as these slogans, advertising messages and other marketing efforts, is to attach certain meanings to cars, something seems to happen to the brand of a car, when enrolled in a CSO. Of course, if car sharing cars were just brand name cars they would not differ much from other cars in society. Therefore the little green monster needs some kind of weapons and tactics to transform the brands of the cars into car sharing cars.

As described earlier, an owner of a certain object is in consumption theory supposed to benefit from the symbolic value of a product. If a consumer owns an expensive car, it may signal that the owner may afford such extravagance as opposed to other consumers and that he/she may therefore be a successful person. For instance, a popular notion is that four-wheel drive SUV's signal status, masculinity and adventurous nature of their owners. Even though the car sharing car fleet consists of world-known brands produced by multi-national corporations, they seem to provide consumers with other symbolic meaning than the meaning offered by the brands. This other type of symbolic meaning

[8] 2005 – 06 – 30: www.mobility.ch; www.majornas-bilkoop.se; www.citycarclub.se

[9] 2007 – 01 – 09: www.opelsverige.com

[10] 2007 – 01 – 09: www.toyota.se

seems to go beyond the product's materiality, its visual surface, or any immaterial values attached to their brand.

The CSO organization communicates a series of values which may be described as quite different to those which the informants describe as favored by commercial interests. The consumers therefore manage to 'detach' themselves from the commercially manufactured meanings of brands. No brand meanings are transferred to the consumers through the CSO; as the consumers do not own the cars, the cars brands do not say anything about their users. Thus, the cooperative ownerships form is used as one tactic to distance consumers from the market. By being a member of the CSO, a consumer makes a statement of wanting to belong to an organization providing an alternative to how the car industry defines the car and rejects the notion of cars as fashion objects. In fact, apart from the financial and practical reasons for joining a car sharing organization, 75 – 80% of Majorna's car sharers state that the ideology behind the CSO are important reasons for joining (Polk, 2000). The car sharing organization does not have to follow the vogues and trends of the market to sell more cars, but may stick to providing cheap, environmentally friendly transportation for its members. Visually, not much is changed with the brand name car when it is enrolled in the CSO; only a sticker with the homepage address is added to the car to show its belonging to the CSO. However, this sticker, costing next to nothing compared with the expensive elaborated branding campaigns, signals that this car is enrolled in the little green monster, and thereby subordinates the brand meaning of the car to the ideological profile of the CSO. Thus, the ideological profile of the CSO combined with a sticker transforms a consumer driving a brand name Ford from someone who has 'felt the difference', into a car sharer who has been attracted to a little green monster aiming to change the world. Thereby the little green monster may be described as hijacking the commercial brand meanings of the car and subordinating them to its own ideological profile.

Majorna – necessary soil for little green monsters?

When the interviewees were asked to describe other car sharers, it seemed clear that it is no coincidence that the car sharing organization began and is still strongly connected to the Majorna residential district in Göteborg. The distribution of the CSO's fleet of cars available to the informants is displayed in the picture below. The picture shows how the fleet of cars is concentrated to the Majorna residential district and to the adjacent residential district Linné.

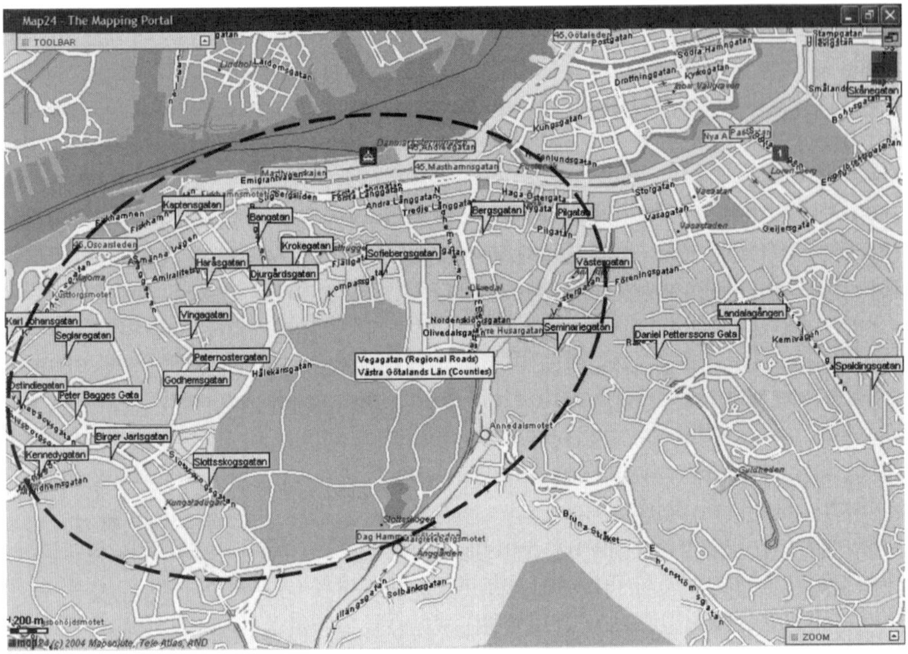

The distribution of cars over western Göteborg, the circle indicates the Majorna- Linné area

Most of the informants described the people who lived in Majorna as having some sort of environmental profile, or interest. In addition the informants said that Majorna residents were not oriented towards money and career but more towards other, inner, values. For example, most of the informants described a Majorna resident as someone who likes to live in sync with nature and the environment. A male informant also described an interesting Majorna stereotype:

When I was working as an intern at the city planning office a few years ago my boss asked where I lived and then she said something I had not thought about; yes those are the people with bikes and bike helmets and first I was like what? But then when I thought about it, it's true, to a large extent. (M, early 40s, CS)

Of course, if a person does not own a car, it is not surprising that a complementary means of transport is important. The bike can, however, also be said to be an important symbol for the environmental movement. The bike is often mentioned in green discourses as a highly energy efficient means of personal transportation (Ottosson and Ottosson, 1998; Lundgren, 1999). In addition, the nature of bike transportation agrees with the values of the green movement. The bike is a slow means of transportation, allowing the biker to enjoy the surroundings in which he/she travels. The bike also allows the rider to feel a connection to nature by the exposure to the elements, even though this exposure might not always be a pleasant experience, considering the cold, rain and wind it may bring. The stereotypical biker described by the informant can serve as a metaphor thus giving the reader an impression of the environmentally affiliated residents of Majorna.

Typical housing of the type "landshövdingehus" in Majorna
Photographer: Karoline Axelson

The Majorna residents were also described as non-materialistic and as people who are for cooperative and collective ideas. One female informant is an illustrative example as she is a member of the association for outdoor life, a cooperative daycare center and lives in a cooperative apartment building. She also gave a representative description of how the informants' accounts reflected the Majorna neighborhood culture:

> It's this thing with solidarity, communality not to... I mean, "right" for me represents private ownership and freedom, while "left" is represented by shared responsibility and here we help one another and some type of "left" wish-wash. To have a little group which gathers, attends meetings and takes turns washing the car and has discussions.

Are we going to buy a new car or not? And if so, which kind should we have? A new car, a sports car or a practical, pure, clean, bi-fuel or... And that is... "green" and it is "left" and it is voluntary associations. (...) I also think that you are quite "pro" the local community. The car sharing organization has cars in other parts of town than Majorna... But it is ... It's not a coincidence that it started in Majorna. There is a lot of local patriotism here. People feel loyal to their community and it's alive and if you go to a café, you go to the café around the corner, and if you go shopping you go shopping here. (F, late 30s, CS)

The many projects founded by residents in Majorna can be seen as the result of how the Majorna neighborhood culture focuses on communal ideas and shared responsibilities that require relationships between the residents. In the context of Majorna's neighborhood culture, the car sharing organization can be seen as a part of a context which questions how our society should be constructed and what it should be like. In the following quote a female car sharer contrasts the many projects founded by the Majorna residents to an experienced diminishing range of choices.

I think it's such a pity that everything is run by the big companies (...) just look at 7-Eleven that I totally boycott since I'm so pissed, frankly, at the way they take over every newsstand in the city. (...) The whole town has the exact same smell, it's the same pastry everywhere and I think it is disgusting and appalling that there can't be any variety (...) and it's not just 7-Eleven, it's other chains as well (...) and it wipes out what little production we still have here in Sweden, things are transported from far away and everything is uniform and it's incredibly boring that everything is so uniform, so uninteresting, and that everybody should like the same things. Terrible. And it's the same with these very big corporations (...) I saw on TV that Findus has now been bought by (...) Nestlé which is such a huge, huge company and now the jars of children's food read Nestlé instead of Findus, I don't like that at all. (F, early 30s, CS)

Several other informants concurred with the view that multi-national retail chains are wiping out perceived differences and making things 'boring' and 'uniform'. The small-scale alternatives of individually owned newsstands are seen as providing diversity, which this informant seems to prefer. The step to share cars, according to many of the informants, requires some kind of 'left-wing mindset'. Many of the informants also believed that these values had led to the many projects founded by residents and voluntary associations that flourish in Majorna, like cooperative daycare, housing and car sharing. The car sharing organization is not a single consumption practice that has emerged by coincidence, but is a part of a range of cooperative alternatives that have been created by Majorna residents. These alternatives can all be seen as creating little monsters in the form of alternatives to the commercialized products and services offered by the market.

The presence of a Majorna neighborhood culture, may explain why a little green monster was born and raised, and perhaps it was also necessary soil for it to grow into a flourishing network employing their guerilla tactics to challenge the black boxes of the car industry. However, as previously displayed in the map the CSO monster has also largely stayed within the borders of this particular neighborhood and its special culture. Of course, some limits to car sharing are quite obvious. CSO's fit best into a metropolitan geographical context as many households may be recruited in a small geographical area in cities, allowing households to be close to their nearest vehicle. As the advantages of car sharing of low costs, high convenience and so forth seems to be so great to consumers, there must be a reason that this little green monster has not spread. Just think about the number of parking spaces that would be saved if a large share of a metropolitan population would start sharing cars. Why has such a great concept not spread in big cities all over the world, revolutionizing the way consumers use cars?

The limits of car sharer enrollment

The arguments provided by green ideology for people to consume more green may touch our hearts and souls. In fact, Swedes have been measured as having very favorable attitudes towards the environment and actions to make society more environmentally friendly such as legislation etc. Yet, only a fraction of the goods that are sold are ecologically friendly alternatives. For instance, 2 – 3% of the provisions sold were eco-labeled in 2003 [11]. Even if the growth rates of ethically labeled goods are high, they are increasing from very small numbers. This may indicate that although consumers may want a more sustainable world, there are hindrances for them to do so. In fact, most of the informants interviewed for my dissertation would like to live more environmentally friendly than they do. However, they also stated that their wishes came in conflict with the reality of everyday life. Environmentally friendly alternatives were described as more expensive, less available and of poorer quality than their non-environmentally friendly counterparts (Jonsson, 2006).

The problems for consumers have to do with the fact that almost all goods are not designed to be environmentally friendly. As most of the products and

[11] 2004 – 04 – 10: www.konsumentverket.se

services we use in everyday life are not environmentally friendly it is much easier for us to 'just go with the flow', than to choose a more expensive alternative, requiring effort from the consumer and sometimes even perceived as having lower quality than their less environmentally friendly counterparts. Latour (1992) would perhaps say that the non-environmentally friendly network of society is dominant, as most of our options are not designed with environmental protection taken into consideration. Thereby, our ways of doing things in consumer society is firmly set into durable material structures making it hard for us to change our ways. Thus, the network of mainstream everyday life of non-organic goods provides resistance of a massive scale. The network is hard to break because the massive pressure from all the non-environmentally friendly alternatives makes it very durable. The small guerilla warfare provided by little green monsters, may be able to question the system of mainstream non-ecological goods, but will it be able to break it up and replace it?

At a first glance the little green monster of CSO's seems to be a great concept providing a new pathway to a more sustainable future. Considering the traffic problems in densely populated European metropolitan areas and the governmental cost for parking etc., CSO's provide a cost-cutting opportunity. Considering the great advantages of car sharing it might seem strange that they have not 'enrolled' more actants to their growing network faster. Also, considering that car sharing is cheaper and at least reported to be more convenient than owning a car it does not seem to be suffering from the same problems as the eco-labeled provisions mentioned earlier. If car sharing is so great then why do we not all sell our cars and join? That would be the rational thing to do!

The challenges to the growth of the car sharing network seem to be rooted in their very foundation, the ideological criticism of the car. Green solutions and alternatives are not always seen very positively, CSO's have been described as a marginal phenomenon, awkward to use and only appealing to environmentally friendly consumers (Siwe, 2004). Green advocates often try to persuade people to live more green by using different 'have to's', we have to use cars less and bike more, we 'have to' recycle etc. (Lundgren, 1999). The usual strategy is to inform people on what they ought to do, and saying that it doesn't take that much effort. If judging by the results in this study, this is not a very good strategy if wanting to get people to act in certain ways. Even if the car sharers were ideologically convinced of the benefits of consuming 'green', and had joined the car sharing organization as a part of their strive, most of the informants made compromises with their green ideology when consuming. The reason was simply that it was too costly and time consuming to think about how we consume all the time. The conclusion I have drawn from this is that faith is not always enough even for the salvaged.

Also, if considering the social meaning of being a member in a car sharing organization, many people in consumer society might not want to be identified as being part of a green little monster. The phenomena of consumers choosing to restrict consumption can be traced to the counter culture of the 1970's. The green wavers of the 1970's may be seen as a stereotype which for many people embody the green idealist. The green wavers often wanted to abandon society and its overly complex structure, return to the good life and strived to live in harmony with nature. According to Wessling (1983) the utopian dreams of leading a simple life often collided with the harsh reality of the labor-intense countryside life for Swedish green wavers. The green wavers were not entirely positively looked upon and were often mocked for their naïve perception of country life. Daydreamers, idealists and parasites are labels that often have been associated with the consumers pursuing the countercultural ideals of the 1970's. Perhaps the unwillingness to identify oneself as green has to do with an image of the green as utopian, out of touch with reality and too idealistic.

Holt (1997) describes that interpretations of consumption practices are separated by symbolic boundaries, which may be detected where interpretations are incompatible or collide. The green ideology inscribed in our CSO monster and in the Majorna neighborhood culture, might act as such a symbolic boundary. The consumers who sympathize with such an ideology can quite easily take on the symbolic value of the CSO. However, there are also other interpretations of cars, not to mention consumption, in consumer society. For instance, driving a car can be an almost sensual experience, at least if being a car lover like myself; enjoying the luxurious sense of leather in a car seat, the thrill of speed and excitement when stepping on the accelerator and listening to the sweet sound of strength from all the horsepower under the hood. Those who criticize cars often underestimate such strong emotional attachments to something as profane as a material possession, a car. The materiality of the car, its design and its nature may be so important for some consumers that they will not be willing to give their fashion item up for a membership in a CSO. Perhaps, they also want to be able to attach the symbolic value of a brand to themselves and may see this as quite unproblematic compared to the car sharers.

The existence of a symbolic boundary would leave the car sharing organization open only to those who agree to the symbolic significance of the CSO.

As long as the CSO is a little green monster, some groups will not want to become members but will see the political connections of the CSO as a disadvantage, or perhaps even a deal-breaker. The Majorna neighborhood culture might be necessary soil for the CSO, however also work as a delimiting to people not comfortable with this neighborhood culture. Therefore the green profile of the CSO might work as a delimiting symbolic boundary sealing off those consumers not wanting to belong to such an organization. Perhaps therefore the fertile soil of the green ideology inherent in the Majorna neighborhood culture has become an obstacle for the further expansion of the CSO monster.

Is our little green monster changing colors?

Some of the informants described that there were members of the CSO as not having a profound ideological commitment. A few of the informants also denounced themselves as being fundamentally green:

> I believe that all of us walk around looking for (...) the eco-labeled products on the shelves, but then you don't have to overdo either (...), like I have this friend NN who overdoes it, she has to go to this shop far, far away to get those special eggs because she knows they are good. (...) When you make restrictions (...) which erodes the quality of life, I could not take those kinds of restrictions, but I gladly put in some effort and try my best to contribute, but it has to be a sensible restriction on the quality of life." (...) In some ways I guess I am a typical car sharer, (...) I have the membership to save money (...) when I'm out talking about CSO's many get a bit surprised when they ask me what I do (a prosecuting attorney). But that is probably because they don't know what the CSO is about, maybe you see these bearded guys in Helly-Hansen [12] fleece sweaters in front of you, (...) but it doesn't work that way any more, that's how it used to be. (...) (M, mid 30's CS)

This informant clearly distances himself from the green 'bearded guys in fleece sweaters'. He takes a stand and declares that car sharing is not about green fundamentalism or ideology. That is something of the past according to him. The development towards members that are primarily not joining for ideological reasons is also described by another female informant. She stated that she joined partly because of the ideology and partly because it is a good way to have access to a car when she needs it. When asked if she could identity herself with the ideological type of car sharer she answered:

[12] An outdoor brand

> I think the environment is important and that you should drive as little as possible, especially in the town center where there are a lot of alternatives and so on. And I'm ok with having to put in some voluntary work for the association, there are many new members that think you should do as little as possible to achieve maximum utility from the membership (. . .) and in a way I can relate to such an attitude, cause I'm also a little lazy, but I think it's (the CSO) such a good idea, that it's worth it. (F, early 40s, CS)

This informant differentiated herself from 'the pure-hearted idealists' in the car sharing organization. She referred to them as 'really great in some senses' but subject to change, wanting everything to stay the same in the CSO, proud and reluctant to make adjustments from the original idea behind the CSO. The new members on the other hand are of a different kind, not having the ideological commitment but viewing car sharing as a solution to a practical problem. Thus, it seems that our little green monster is considering taking a new pathway away from its ideological green childhood. All members did not welcome this development. One male car sharer firmly stated that he didn't like the recent development of Majorna's CSO. He described himself as an orthodox and had decided to leave the Majorna's CSO when the organization bought cars that according to his opinion were too expensive and status-oriented. The cars in question were a Toyota Prius, an environmentally friendly car and a Volkswagen Golf.

He said that he dislikes the expansion of the CSO and even that he sees it as a threat to the entire organization. According to this male car sharer the CSO's are based on closeness between individuals who feel responsible for each other, which the expansion of the CSO makes impossible as it leads to anonymity and alienation. He viewed the new internet-based booking system with scepticism and said that it's not good that you can't see who had the car before you rent it. According to his view, this more anonymous system lets people get away with leaving the cars not in proper condition – unclean, with a bump or just out of gas.

It seems that our CSO monster is at a crossroad. On one hand we have the members advocating the gains of being a member in a commercial, high-service grade CSO. They argue that if living in a metropolitan area this makes the advantages so great for consumers that they choose this alternative over owning a car. On the other hand, we have members fighting to keep their monster at war, opening up the black boxes of consumer society and questioning the market system. Provided that the CSO's have a high-service degree car sharing it enrolls members simply by solving everyday problems for consumers in metropolitan areas more efficiently than a privately owned car. As the CSO is enrolling more and more actants due to its more effective solution to private transportation, it may be transforming itself from an ideological alternative into a service product among others in a commercial market. As we have seen, some of the car sharers welcome such a development, while others see it as undesirable. However, this change may not be in the hands of the original ideologically oriented members any more, but rather of the future members of the CSO. As the non-ideological actants are enrolled in this monster, they not only grow in numbers but also in influence. The CSO seems to have gained a life of its own and is perhaps not possible to control for those who started it. Some of the more ideologically oriented members may quit as described above. However as long as the monster keeps enrolling more members than it loses the monster grows in numbers of actants, and consequently in power and influence.

The re-invention of a CSO from ideological to 'neutral' is the typical case of the development and growth of a CSO, according to Per Schillander[13]. He described that a CSO often starts out with members who have a strong environmental ideological profile. In a second stage people join as the cost is so low. When the CSO has grown and the service degree provided by the CSO is high, like Mobility in Switzerland with over 60,000 users, members join primarily because of the convenience of car sharing, according to Schillander. As previously mentioned, car sharers joining for the sake of convenience might have different values than the founders of the organizations, and may not be interested as being viewed as part of a 'green' organization. The green ideology might then in fact work as a delimiting symbolic boundary for the organization's ability to attract new members to enroll within the car sharing organization's network. Which direction our CSO monster is going to choose is still a tale to be told. If the little green monster has truly gotten a life on its own, wanting to attract members beyond its green symbolic boundaries, it might decide to abandon its fertile soil of green ideology. A pity, perhaps, however the environmentally friendly effects of the consumer practice of car sharing will spread to its new members and a larger network. But perhaps, just that, spreading environmentally friendly behavior on to more consumers, was the intention of the green ideology all along?

[13] Interview with Per Schillander, who works with car sharing at the Swedish road administration 2003 – 01 – 13

Afterword

Alison J. CLARKE

Little Monsters offers a timely empirical and theoretical antidote to traditional commodity chain-type approaches that once dominated consumer studies with their juxtaposition of 'hard' economy and 'soft' culture set in a strictly linear model. Incorporating extraordinary attention to detail, from the half-eaten hamburgers of a McDonald's children's birthday party to the hybrid /non-human 'thongs' that merges with human 'girl' (thus engendering the transition to feminine teenagedom) we are offered a view of material culture that once and for all overturns a hierarchy of meaning in which 'significance' begins with production and culminates in consumption. Here nodes of significances are inseparable from one another; commodities and practices are embedded in networks that are fluid, malleable but ultimately unpredictable.

Over the last two decades, the work of Latour and Actor-Network Theory has implicitly informed the study of commercial cultures. Little Monsters, however, *explicitly* embraces ANT taking to task any prior notion of consumer objects, practices and media as discrete entities. In this collection the everyday, the mundane, the quaint and the straightforwardly weird and often absurd aspects of popular consumer culture (including car sharing organisations, wedding memory boxes, do-it-yourself print-out paper models) are interrogated using a theoretical approach that obliterates pre-conceived hierarchies of cultural meaning and asserts consumption instead as moments of assemblage. And it is the study of the minutiae of everyday consumer practice and the intersections of corporations and markets into everyday social worlds that Little Monsters perhaps makes its greatest contribution.

The valorization of everyday life has been at the core of the sociological, anthropological and historical move to consumption that has taken place over the last three decades; resulting in an understanding of political economy through the detail of the quotidian. Material Culture studies and Actor-Network Theory, along with the re-invigoration of ethnographic inquiry, have simultaneously sought to relocate the specificity of the 'thing' (as a process as much as an object) at the fore of inter-disciplinary academic inquiry.

The tracing of ephemeral objects and commercial practices has an established Marxist-based historiography from Benjamin's *Arcades Project* (1999) to Haug's *Critique of Commodity Aesthetics* (1986). Historical studies, such as Mintz's classic monograph *Sweetness and Power: The Place of Sugar in Modern History* (1985) tackled the macro-narratives of commodity cultures and political economy. But as academic language has shifted from one of 'totalities' to one incorporating metaphors of 'networks', so too the critique of capitalism has complexified.

It is no coincidence that the theoretical move towards consumption over the last decades has been coupled with a corporate move towards ethnographic and qualitative research in the making and dissemination of products. While marketing companies utilize increasingly grassroots techniques, such 'anonymous advertising' in the form of staged brand-conversations made to be 'accidentally' over-heard in public places, the demand for academic approaches that debunk the binaries of culture and economy, and take on the convergences of marketing, economics and social lives, is critical. The contributors to *Little Monsters* engage simultaneously with scientific studies of culture *and* issues of marketing without apology.

From home-decoration show rooms to the fashion accessories of young girls, Little Monsters, those potential subversive assemblages of agencies and networks, reveal how politics and ethics arise in the spaces previously condemned as apolitical. This anthology offers us a new and invigorating way forward in the study of a practice so embedded that even to identify it as a discrete entity- 'consumption' – is surely now redundant.

References

Akrich, Madeleine and Latour, Bruno 2000 (1992), 'A Convenient Vocabulary for the Semiotic of Human and Nonhuman Actors', Bijker, Wiebe and John Law (eds) *Shaping Technology. Building Society Studies in Sociotechnological Change*, Cambridge: MA:MIT Press.

Alanen, Leena (1992), *Modern childhood? Exploring the 'child question' in sociology'* Institute for educational research. Publication series A. Research reports 50, University of Jyväskylä.

– (2001), 'Explorations in generational analysis', L. Alanen and B. Mayall (eds), *Conceptualizing child-adult relations*, London and New York: Routledge/Falmer Press.

Anderson, Richard, L. 2000, *American Muse. Anthropological Excursions into Art and Aesthetic'* Kansas: Kansas City Art Institute.

Appadurai, Arjun (1986), 'Introduction: commodities and the politics of value', Appadurai Arjun (ed.) *The social life of things: commodities in cultural perspective,* Cambridge: Cambridge Univ. Press.

Ariès, Philippe (1962), *Centuries of Childhood,* New York: Vintage Books.

Arnould, Eric J. and Thompson, Craig J. (2005), 'Consumer Culture Theory (CCT): Twenty Years of Research', *Journal of Consumer Research.*Vol. 31 Issue 4.

Aslaksen, F., Bergh, S., Bringa, O. R. & Heggem, E. K. (1997), *Universal design. Planning and Design for All,* Report, Oslo: The Norwegian State Council on Disability.

Bachelard, Gaston (1969) *The Poetics of Space*, Boston: Beacon Press.

Barthes, Roland (1997),*Mythologies*, New York: Hill and Wang.

Baudrillard, Jean (1996), *The System of Objects*, London and New York: Verso.

Bauman, Zygmund (2002), *Society under Siege.* London: Polity Press.

Belk, Russel W. (1988), 'Possessions and the extended self', *Journal of Consumer Research* Vol. 15 (September).

– (1995), *Collecting in a Consumer Society,* London and New York: Routledge.

– and Melanie Wallendorf, John F. Sherry Jr. (1991), 'The Sacred and the Profane in Consumer Behavior: Theodicy on the Odyssey', Belk, R.W. (ed.), *Highways and Buyways: Naturalistic Research from the Consumer Behavior Odyssey*, Provo, UT: Association for Consumer Research.

Benjamin, Walter (1999), *The Arcades Project*, Cambridge, Mass.: Belknap Press.

Berggren Torell, Viveka (2004), 'Adults and children debating sexy girl's clothes', H. Brembeck, B. Johansson and J. Kampmann (eds), *Beyond the competent child. Exploring contemporary childhoods in the Nordic welfare societies*, København: Samfunnsforlaget.

Bergquist, Magnus and Ljungberg, Jan (2001), 'The Power of Gifts: Organizing social relationships in open source communities', *Info Systems Journal* 11.

Bloom, Michelle (2003), *Waxworks. The culture of an obsession*, Minneapolis and London: University of Minneapolis Press.

Bloor, Janet and Sinclair, John D. (2004), *Rubber! Fun, fashion, fetish,* London: Thames & Hudson.

Boyd, Norman N (2007), *The Model Ship: Her role in history*, Woodbridge.

Brembeck, Helene (2007), *Hem tille Mc Donald's*, Stockholm: Bokförlaget Carlsson.

Brembeck, Helene (2004), 'Pinocchio Meets Jafar: The Wonders of the Happy Meal Toys', H. Brembeck, B. Johansson and J. Kampmann (eds), *Beyond the competent child. Exploring contemporary childhoods in the Nordic welfare societies*, København: Samfunnsforlaget.

(2005), 'Home to McDonald's. Upholding the family dinner by the help of McDonald's', *Food, Culture, and Society* 2005/3.

– and Johansson, Barbro and Kampmann, Jan (eds) (2004), *Beyond the competent child. Exploring contemporary childhoods in the Nordic welfare societies*, København: Samfunnsforlaget.

– and Ekström, Karin M. (eds) (2004), *Elusive Consumption,* Oxford and New York: Berg.

– and Ekström, Karin M. (eds) (2005), *Elusive Consumption in retrospect. Report from the conference.* CFK-rapport 2005:01. Göteborgs universitet, Centrum för konsumentvetenskap, *www.cfk.gu.se*.

Bringéus, Nils-Arvid (1986), *Människan som kulturvarelse; En introduktion till etnologin*, Malmö: Liber Förlag

Brown, Steven D and Rose Capdevila (1999), 'Perpetuum mobile: substance, food and the sociology of translations', John Law and John Hassard (eds) *Actor Network Theory and After*, Oxford: Blackwell.

Butler, Judith (1990), *Gender trouble. Feminism and the subversion of identity*, New York and London: Routledge.

– (1993), *Bodies that matter. On the discursive limits of 'sex'*, New York and London: Routledge.

Buttgereit, Jörg, Ecke, Thomas and Engel, Rainer F. (2000), *Nightmares in Plastic*, München: Bellevill-Verlag.

Callon, Michel (1999), 'Actor-network theory – the market test', J. Law and J. Hassard (eds), *Actor Network Theory and after*, Oxford: Blackwell.

– and Latour, Bruno (1981), 'Unscrewing the big Leviathan: How actors macro-structure reality and how sociologists help them to do so', Knorr-Cetina, K. and Cicouvel, A.V. (eds), *Advances in social theory and methodology: towards an integration of micro and macro-sociology*, Boston, MA, London: Routledge.

Carter, Sandra (1992), *Vårt bröllop. En minnesbok'* Örebro: Libris.

Carter, Simon & Mike Michael (2004), 'Here comes the Sun: Shedding Light on the Cultural Body', Helen Thomas and Jamilah Ahmed (eds) *Cultural Bodies. Ethnography and Theory,* Oxford: Blackwell.

Castells, Manuel (1997), *The information age: Economy, society & culture – The power of identity*, Oxford: Blackwell.

Clarke, Alison J. (2001), 'The Aesthetics of Social Aspiration', Miller, Daniel (ed.) *Home possessions: material culture behind closed doors'* Oxford: Berg.

– and Miller, Daniel (2002), 'Fashion and anxiety', *Fashion Theory*, volume 6, issue 2.

Cochoy, Frank (2004), 'Is the Modern Consumer a Buridan's Donkey? Product Packaging and Consumer Choice', Ekström, Karin M. and Helene Brembeck (eds), *Elusive Consumption.* Oxford: Berg.

– (2005), 'Publicizing Goldilocks' Choice at the Supermarket. The Political Work of Shopping Packs, Carts and Talk', Latour, Bruno and Weibel, Peter (eds), *Making things public: atmospheres of democracy,* Cambridge, Mass.: MIT Press.

Coleman, Roger (1999), 'Inclusive design – Design for All', William Green and Patrick Jordan (eds), *Human Factors in Product Design. Current Practice and Future Trends'* London: Taylor and Francis.

Cooper, Robert (1997), 'The visibility of social systems', Hetherington, Kevin and Munro, Rolland (eds), *Ideas of difference: social spaces and the labour of division,* Oxford, Blackwell.

Czarniawska, Barbara (2004), *On Time, Space and Action Nets.* GRI-rapport 2004:5. Göteborg: Gothenburg Research Institute (GRI).

– and Joerges, Bernward (1996), 'Travels of Ideas', Czarniawska, Barbara and Sevon, Guje (eds), *Translating organizational change'* Berlin: de Gruyter.

– and Sevón, Guje (eds) (1996), *Translating organizational change,* Berlin: de Gruyter.

Danet, Brenda (2001), *Cyberplay. Communicating Online*, Oxford: Berg.

Dawson, Graham (1994) *Soldier Heroes. British adventure, empire and the imagining of masculinities*, London and New York: Routledge.

De Landa, Manuel (1999), 'Deleuze and the open-ended becoming of the world', http://www.cddc.vt.edu/host/delanda/pages/becoming.htm.

Deleuze, Gilles (1992) 'What is dispositif?', Armstrong, T. J. (ed.) *Michel Foucault, Philosopher*, New York: Routledge.

Di Leonardo, Micaela (1987), 'The Family World of Cards and Holidays: Women, Families and Work of Kinship', *Signs* 12.

Dobers, Peter and Strannegård, Lars (2005), 'Design, Lifestyle and Sustainability. Aesthetic Consumption in a World of Abundance', *Business Strategy and the Environment*, Vol. 14.

Douglas, Mary and Isherwood (Baron 1979), *The World of Goods. Towards an anthropology of consumption*, Suffolk: Allen Lane.

Ek, Richard (2005), 'Mot ett kritiskt perspektiv på servicelandskap – Behovet av Critical Service Management Studies', Corvellec, Hervé and Lindquist (eds) *Servicemötet,* Malmö: Liber.

Ekström, Karin M. (2005), 'Ritualer och sakraliserade glassamlingar' [Rituals and sacralized glass collections], *Kulturella Perspektiv*, Svensk etnologisk tidskrift, nr 2, vol. 14.

– (2004), OSETT, *Glas ur privata samlingar 12/12 2004 – 30/1 2005* [UNSEEN – Glass from private collections 12/12 2004 – 30/1 2005], Smålands museum – Sveriges glasmuseum och Konst- och Bruksglasföreningen.

Ellegaard, Tomas (2004), 'Self-goverance and incompetence: Teachers' construction of "the competent child"', H. Brembeck, B. Johansson and J. Kampmann (eds), *Beyond the competent child. Exploring contemporary childhoods in the Nordic welfare societies*, København: Samfunnsforlaget.

Entwistle, Joan (2000), *The fashioned body: fashion, dress and modern social theory*, Cambridge: Polity Press.

Eurostat: 101, *Statistical Office of the European Commission, Living Conditions in Europe*: Statistical Handbook.

Frønes, Ivar (1995), *Among Peers. On the Meaning of Peers in the Process of Socialization*, Oslo/Stockholm/Copenhagen/Boston: Scandinavian University Press.

Gregson, Nicky, Crewe, Louise and Brooks, Kate (2002), 'Shopping, space, and practice', *Environment and Planning D: Society and Space,* Volume 20.

– and Metcalfe, Alan and Crewe, Louise (forthcoming) 'Identity, mobility and the throwaway society', *Environment and Planning D: Society and Space.*

Gabriel, Yiannis and Lang, Tim (1995), *The Unmanageable Consumer – Contemporary Consumption and its Fragmentation*, London: SAGE.

Gelber, Steven M. (1999), *Hobbies. Leisure and the Culture of Work in America*, New York: Columbia University Press.

Goffman, Erving (1959/1990), *The presentation of self in everyday life*, London: Penguin Books.

Gorb and Dumas (1987), 'Silent design', Margaret Bruce and Rachel Cooper (eds), *Marketing and Design Management,* London: International Thomson Business.

Green, William and Jordan, Patrick (1999), 'Ergonomics, Usability and Product Development', William Green & Patrick Jordan (eds), *Human Factors in Product Design. Current Practice and Future Trends*, London: Taylor and Francis.

Hansson, Lena (2006), *Universal design – a marketable or utopian concept?,* Göteborg: Center for Consumer Science.

Haug, Wolfgang Fritz (1986), *Critique of Commodity Aesthetics: Appearance, Sexualitiy and Advertising in Capitalist Society*, Minneapolis: University of Minnesota Press.

Haraway, Donna (1991), 'A Cyborg manifesto: Science, technology, and socialist-feminism in the late twentieth century', D. Haraway (ed.), *Simians, cyborgs and women: the reinvention of nature*, New York: Routledge.

Hetherington, Kevin (1997), 'In place of geometry: the materiality of place', Hetherington, Kevin and Munro, Rolland (eds) *Ideas of difference: social spaces and the labour of division'* Oxford: Blackwell.

– (1999), 'From Blindness to blindness: museums, heterogenity and the subject', Law, John and Hassard, John (eds) *Actor Network Theory and After'* Oxford: Blackwell.

Hine, Christine (2000), *Virtual Ethnography*, London: Sage.

Hirdman, Anja (2001), *Tilltalande bilder: genus, sexualitet och publiksyn i Veckorevyn och FIB-Aktuellt,* Stockholm: Atlas.

Hirschman, Elizabeth and M. Holbrook (1982), 'Hedonic Consumption: Emerging Concepts, Methods and Propositions', *Journal of Marketing*, Vol.46, No.3.

Holbrook, Morris and E. Hirschman Elizabeth C. (1982), 'The Experiential Aspects of Consumptions: Fantasies, Feelings and Fun,' *Journal of Consumer Research,* September 9.

Holt, Douglas B. (1997), 'Poststructuralist Lifestyle Analysis: Conceptualizing the Social Petterning of Consumption in Postmodernity', *Journal of Consumer Research*, Vol.23, No.4.

Hougaard, Bent (2004), *Curlingföräldrar och servicebarn*' Stockholm: Prisma.

Huldt, Johan (1999), 'De stora utställningarnas tid 1945 – 60', *Svenskt glas*, Stockholm: Wahlström & Widstrand.

Håkansson, Håkan, Harrison, Debbie, Waluszewski, Alexandra (2004), *Rethinking Marketing: A New Understanding of Markets*, Chichester: Wiley cop.

Jackson, Peter, Lowe, Michelle, Miller, Daniel and Mort Frank (eds) (2000), *Commercial Cultures. Economics, Practices, Spaces,* Oxford and New York: Berg.

Jakobsson, Ulf (2002), *Towards more sustainable mobility – exploring success factors for car sharing in Europe*, Lund University.

James, Alison and Prout, Alan (eds) (1997), *Constructing and reconstructing childhood: Contemporary issues in the sociological study of childhood*, London/Bristol: The Falmer Press.

– Jenks, Chris and Prout, Alan (1998), *Theorizing childhood*, Cambridge and New York: Polity Press: Teachers College Press.

Johansson, Barbro (2005), *Brokiga bilder av barns konsumtion: Hur barn och konsumtion framställs i några svenska medier*. CFK-rapport 2005:01a. Göteborgs universitet: Centrum för konsumentvetenskap. *www.cfk.gu.se*

– (2005b), *Barn i konsumtionssamhället,* Stockholm: Norstedts Akademiska Förlag.

Jonsson, Pernilla (2006), *Capturing the elusive simplifier*, Göteborg: Center for Consumer Science.

Jordan, Patrick (1999), 'Inclusive design', William Green & Patrick Jordan (eds), *Human Factors in Product Design. Current Practice and Future Trends,* London: Taylor & Francis.

Kavanagh, Donnacha and Araujo, Luis (1995), 'Chronigami: Folding and Unfolding Time', *Accounting, Management and Information Technologies* 5(2).

Keates, Simeon and Clarkson, John (2004), *Countering design exclusion. An introduction to inclusive design*, London: Springer.

Kiendel, Anthony (2001), 'Little Worlds', Marzolf, Helen *Little Worlds (ed.)*, Regina: Dunlop Art Gallery.

Kitzman, Andreas (2004), *Saved from Oblivion. Documenting the Daily from Diaries to Web Cams,* New York: Peter Lang.

Korsmeyer, Carolyn (2004), *Gender and Aesthetics: An Introduction.* New York: Routledge.

Kotler, Philip and Rath, Alexander (1984), 'Design: A Powerful but Neglected Strategic Tool', *Journal of Business Strategy*, No. 5 (Fall).

Kozinets, Robert V (2002), 'Can Consumers Escape the Market? Emancipatory illuminations from Burning Man', *Journal of Consumer Research,* Vol. 29, No. 1.

Knuts, Eva (2006), *Något gammalt, något nytt – skapandet av bröllopsföreställningar'* Göteborg: Mara.

– (2007), 'Mock Brides, Hen Parties and Weddings, Changes in Time and Space', Terry Gunnel (ed.) *Masks and Mummings in the Nordic Area*, Uppsala: Gustav Adolfs Akademien.

Lai, Albert W. (1995), 'Consumer Values, Product Benefits and Customer Value: A Consumption Behavior Approach', Kardes, Frank R. and Mita Sujan (eds.), *Advances in Consumer Research*, Vol. 20, Provo, UT: Association for Consumer Research.

Lally, Elaine (2002), *At Home with Computers*, Oxford: Berg.

Latour, Bruno (1986), 'The powers of association', Law, John (ed.), *Power, action and belief,* London: Routledge and Kegan Paul.

– (1987), *Science in action: How to follow scientists and engineers through society*, Cambridge: Harvard University Press.

– (1992), 'Teknik är samhället som gjorts hållbart', *Artefaktens återkomst*, Stockholm: Nerenius & Santérus Förlag.

– (1993), *Aramis or the Love of Technology,* Cambridge and London: Harvard University Press.

– (1997), 'Trains of thought – Piaget, formalism and the fifth dimension', *Common Knowledge,* Volume 6, Issue 3.

– (1999), 'On recalling ANT', John Law and John Hassard (eds), *Actor Network Theory and After,* Oxford: Blackwell.

– (1998), *Artefaktens återkomst: Ett möte mellan organisationsteori och tingens sociologi,* Göteborg: Nerenius & Santérus förlag.

– (1999), *Pandora's hope: Essays on the reality of science studies*, Cambridge, Massachussetts, London, England: Harvard University Press.

– (2005), *Reassembling the Social,* Oxford: Oxford University Press.

– and Weibel, Peter (eds) (2005), *Making things public: atmospheres of democracy,* Cambridge, Mass.: MIT Press.

Law, John (1991), *A Sociology of Monsters. Essays on Power, Thechnology and Domination,* London and New York: Routledge.

– (1999), 'After ANT: Complexity, naming and topology', John Law and John Hassard (eds), *Actor Network Theory and After,* Oxford: Blackwell Publishers.

– (2000), 'Objects, Spaces and Others', On-line paper, Centre for Science Studies, Lancaster University. www.lancs.ac.uk/fss/sociology/papers/law-objects-spaces-others.pdf

– and Hassard, John (eds) (1999), *Actor Network Theory and After,* Oxford: Blackwell Publishers.

Lee, Nick (2001), *Childhood and society: Growing up in an age of uncertainty,* Buckingham/Philadelphia: Open University Press.

Lefevbre, Henri (1991/1971), *The production of space,* Oxford: Basil Blackwell.

Leibrock, Cynthia and Terry, James Evan (1999), *Beautiful Universal design – a visual guide*, New York: John Wiley and Sons Inc.

Lindstrom, Martin (2003), *Brandchild: Remarkable Insights into the Minds of Today's Global Kids and their Relationships with Brands*, London and Sterling, VA: Kogan Page.

Lundgren, Lars J. (1999), 'Önskemål och möjligheter', Lundgren, Lars, J. (ed.), *Livsstil och miljö – Värderingar, val, vanor*, Kristianstad: Byggforskningsrådet.

Lury, Celia (1997), *Consumer Culture*, Cornwell, UK: Polity Press.

Löfgren, Orvar and Willim, Robert (eds) (2005), *Magic, Culture and the New Economy,* Oxford and New York: Berg.

Mace, Ronald L. (1998), 'A Perspective on Universal Design', Jan Reagan (ed.),

Published presentation at 'Designing for the 21 Century: An International Conference on Universal Design', June 19, Adaptive Environments.

MacKenzie, Jon (2001), *Perform – or else: From discipline to performance*, London and New York: Routledge.

Majua, Margaret and Weingarten, David (1996), *Souvenir Buildings, Miniature Monuments,* New York: Harry N. Abrahams.

Marcoux, Jean-Sebastien (2001), 'The "Casser Maison" Ritual: Constructing the Self by Emptying the Home', *Journal of Material Culture*, vol. 6: issue 7.

Martin, Emily (1997), 'Citadels and stringfigures', Akhil Gupta and James Ferguson (eds), *Anthropological Locations.* Berkeley: University of California Press.

Mathiesen Hjemdahl, Kirsti (2003*), Tur-retur temapark – oppdragelse, opplevelse, kommers,*Kristiansand: Høyskoleforlaget.

McCracken, Grant (1986), 'Culture and Consumption: A Theoretical Account of the Structure and Movement of the Cultural Meaning of Consumer Goods', *Journal of Consumer Research,* vol. 13 (June).

– (1988), 'The Evocative Power of Things. Consumer Goods and the Preservation of Hopes and Ideals', Grant McCracken (ed.) *Culture and Consumption. New Approaches to the Symbolic Character of Consumer Goods and Activities*, Bloomington: Indiana University Press.

– (1988), *Culture and Consumption: new approaches to the symbolic character of consumer goods and activities*, Bloomington: Indiana University Press.

– (1989), 'Homeyness: a cultural account of the constellation of consumer goods and meaning', *Interpretive consumer research.*

Meikle, Jeffrey L. (1995), 'Domesticating Modernity: Ambivalence and Appropriation', Kaplan, Wendy (ed.) *Designing Modernity. The arts of reform and persuasion 1885 – 1945,* London: Thames and Hudson.

Meyer, Werner and Damsch-Wiehager Renate (1988), *Züge Züge. Die Eisenbahn in der zeitgeössischen Kunst*, Cantz Verlag.

Michael, Mike (2000), *Reconnecting Culture, Technology and Nature,* London and New York: Routledge.

Miller, Daniel (ed.) (1997), *Material Cultures. Why some things matter,* Chicago: Chicago University Press.

– (1998), *A Theory of Shopping,* Cambridge: Polity Press.

– (2000), 'The Birth of Value', Jackson, Peter, Lowe, Michelle, Miller, Daniel and Mort Frank (eds) *Commercial Cultures. Economics, Practices, Spaces,* Oxford and New York: Berg.

Mintz, Sidney W. (1985), *Sweetness and Power: The Place of Sugar in Modern History*, New York: Princeton University Press.

Mobility (2005), *Annual report 2004 of Mobility*, Switzerland.

Mol, Annemari and Law, John (1994), 'Regions, Networks and Fluids: Anaemia and social topology', *Social Studies of Science* Volume 24, Issue 4.

Monö, Rune (1997), *Design for Product Understanding. The Aesthetics of Design from a Semiotic Approach*, Stockholm: Liber AB.

Moon, Karen (2005), *Modelling Messages, The Architect and the Model,* New York: Monachelli Press.

Moschis, George P., Lee, Euehun and Mathur, Anil (1997), 'Targeting the mature market: opportunities and challenges', *Journal of Consumer Marketing*, vol. 14, no. 4.

Moser, Ingunn and Law, John (1999), 'Good passages, bad passages', John Law and John Hassard (eds), *Actor Network Theory and after*. Oxford: Blackwell.

Mulvey, Laura (1989), *Visual and other pleasures*, Basingtoke: Macmillan.

Munro, Rolland (1997), 'Ideas of difference: stability, social spaces and labour of division', Hetherington, Kevin and Munro, Rolland (eds) *Ideas of difference: social spaces and the labour of division*' Oxford: Blackwell.

Mörck, Magnus (2006), 'From Analogue to Digital (and back). Collecting in an Internet community', *European Advances in Consumer Research*, vol. VII.

– and Tullberg, Maria (2004), *Catwalk för direktörer. Bolagsstämman – en performativ performans av maskuliniteter*, CFK-Rapport 2004:02a. Göteborgs universitet, Centrum för konsumentvetenskap, *www.cfk.gu.se*.

Nievergelt, Dieter (2001), *Architectur aus Papier. Häuser, Kirchen, Monumente: eine Welt im Kleinen*, Lausanne: Musée historique de Lausanne.

Norman, Donald A. (1998), *Psychology of everyday things*, Cambridge, Massachusetts: MIT Press.

Ostroff, Elaine (2001), 'Universal design: The new paradigm', Wolfgang Preiser and Elaine Ostroff (eds), *Universal design Handbook*, New York: McGraw-Hill.

Otnes, Cele C. and Pleck, Elisabeth H. (2003), *Cinderella Dreams: The allure of the Lavish Weddings,* Berkley, Los Angeles, London: University of California Press.

Ottoson, Mats and Ottosson, Åsa (1998), *Lagom är bäst! På spaning efter en hållbar livsstil*, Naturskyddsföreningens årsbok 1998, Värnamo: Naturskyddsföreningens Förlag.

Papanek, Victor (1984), *Design for the real world*, second edition, London: Butler & Tanner.

Paulsson, Jan (2000), "Universal design – ett grundläggande perspektiv i arkitektur och formgivning", Project description EIDD Sverige, Education group.

Peers, Juliette (2004), *The Fashion Doll. From Bebe Jumeau to Barbie*, Oxford: Berg.

Pepperell, Robert (2003), *The posthuman condition. Consciousness beyond the brain,* Bristol: Itellect Books.

Petersson, Magdalena (2003), *Identitetsföreställningar: Performance, normativitet och makt ombord på SAS och AirHoliday,* Göteborg: Mara.

Phillips, Phoebe (1987), *The Encyclopedia of glass*, London: Spring Books.

Pickering, Andrew (1993), The Mangle of Practice: Agency and Emergence in the Sociology of Science', *American Journal of Sociology* 99(3).

Pieske, Christa (1984), *Das ABC des Luxuspapier,* Berlin: Reimer.

Pinteau, Pascal (2005), *Special Effects. An Oral History*, New York: Harry N. Abrahams Inc.

Pleck, Elizabeth H. (2000), *Celebrating the Family. Ethnicity, Consumer Culture, and Family Rituals,* Cambridge, Mass.: Harvard University Press.

Polk, Merritt (2000), *Majornas Bilkoperativ – ett föredöme i bilsamhället – Car sharing in Sweden: A case study of the implementation of an internet booking system in Majornas car cooperative in Göteborg*, Unpublished report produced on assignment from Vägverket, Göteborg.

Prout, Alan (2005), *The future of childhood*, London and New York: RoutledgeFalmer Press.

Quart, Alissa (2003), *Branded: The buying and selling of teenagers*, London: Arrow.

Qvortrup, Jens (1987), *The sociology of childhood*, Barndomsprojektet 2/87, University Centre of South Jutland.

– (1994), *Barn halva priset: Nordisk barndom i samhällsperspektiv,* Esbjerg: Sydjysk Universitetsforlag.

Reimer, Suzanne and Leslie, Deborah (2004), 'Identity, Consumption and the Home', *Home Cultures*, Volume 1, Number 2.

Rhodin, Petra (2001), *Resurseffektivisering ur ett brukarperspektiv*, Institutionen för människa – tekniksystem, Göteborg: Chalmers Tekniska Högskola.

Richins, Marsha L. (1994), 'Special Possessions and the Expression of Material Values', *Journal of Consumer Research*, Vol. 21 (December).

Rogers, Mary F (1998), *Barbie Culture*, London: Sage.

Rollins, Nita (1991), 'Something borrowed, something taped: Video Nuptials', *Wide Angle* 13(2).

Rosell, Gustaf (1994), 'The Human Dimension', T. Dahlin, D. Mascanzoni, G. Rosell, and L. Svengren (eds), *The Human Dimension*, Swedish Industrial Design, Italia: Edizioni Bolis.

Russell, Rachel and Tyler, Melissa (2004), *Branding and bricolage: gender and tweenage consumption in transitional spaces*. Paper presented at the conference Pluridsciplinary perspectives on child and teen consumption, Universite de Poitiers, 25 – 26th March 2004.

Rybczynski, Witold (1988), *Home: a short history of an idea*‘ London: Heinemann.

Salomonsson, Karin (2006), ‘En minnesvärd måltid’, Burstedt, Anna, Cecilia Fredriksson and Håkan Jönsson (eds), *Mat. Genealogi och gestaltning.* Lund: Studentlitteratur.

Sandon, John (1999), *Starting to Collect Antique Glass*, England: Antique Collectors’ Club Ltd.

Schor, Juliet B. (2004), *Born to buy: the commercialized child and the new consumer culture*, Scribner.

Schroeder, Jonathan (2002), *Visual consumption*, London: Routledge.

Serre, Michel (1982), *The Parasite*‘ Baltimore, Md: John Hopkins University Press.

Sherry, John F. Jr. (2000), ‘Place, Technology, and Representation’, *Journal of Consumer Research* Vol. 27, Issue 2.

Simmel Georg (1971), *On individuality and social forms: selected writings*, Chicago: Univ. of Chicago P.

Siwe, Malin (2004), ‘Minimalt intresse för att dela bilar’, *Metro* 2004 – 03 – 25.

Slater, Don (1997), *Consumer Culture & Modernity*, Cambridge: Polity Press.

Smith, Albert C. (2004), *Architectural Model as Machine*. Amsterdam: Elsevier.

Sparke, Penny (1987), *Design in Context*, London: Bloomsbury.

Sparke, Penny (2004), *An introduction to design and culture [1900 to the present],* second edition, London: Routledge.

Speerling, Daniel and Shaheen, Susan (1999), *Carsharing – niche market or new pathway*, KFB-rapport, 2000:15, Sweden: Kommunikationsforskningsberedningen.

Stölting, Siegfrid (1989), *Schiffe aus Papier*, Bremen: Worpsweder Verlag.

Sutherland, Ann and Thompson, Beth (2003), *Kidfluence: The Marketer’s Guide to Understanding and Reaching Generation Y – Kids, Tweens, and Teens*, New York/London/New Delhi/Sydney: McGraw-Hill.

Thackara, John (1988), *Design after Modernity – beyond the object*, Great Britain: Thames and Hudson.

Thrift, Nigel (1996), *Spatial Formations*‘ London: Sage Publications.

– (2006), ‘Space’, *Theory, Culture & Society* Vol 23, Issue 2 – 3.

Tolkien, J.R.R. (1954), *The Fellowship of the Ring'* London: George Allen and Unwin.

Urban Glen H. and John R. Hauser, (1993), *Design and Marketing of New Products*, 2nd. ed. Prentice Hall, Englewood Cliffs, N.J.

Ward, Arthur (1999), *Airfix. Celebrating 50 years of the greatest plastic kits in the world*, London: HarperCollins.

Welch, Polly (1995), *Strategies for Teaching Universal Design*, Boston: Adaptive Environments Center.

Whiteley, Nigel (1993), *Design for Society*, London: Reaktion Books Ltd.

Woodham, Jonathan (1997), *Twentieth-Century Design,* New York: Oxford University Press.

Wærdahl, Randi (2003), *Learning by consuming: consumer culture as a condition for socialization and every day life at the age of 12*, Rapport 4:2003, Institutt for sosiologi og samfunnsgeografi, Universitetet i Oslo.

Wenzer, Jakob (2002), *Maskinisk Barndom – Ett sammanförande av fälten barndomsforskning och teknologikritik genom Gilles Deleuze och Félix Guattari,* D-uppsats, Etnologiska institutionen, Göteborgs universitet.

Wessling, Ulla (1983), 'Leva nära naturen. Om det underförstådda i naturens budskap i Svenska livsstilar – Om naturen som resurs och symbol', Hjort, Anders (ed.), *Svenska livsstilar – Om naturen som resurs och symbol,* Stockholm: Liberförlag.

Östergaard, Per, James A. Fitchett and Christian Janzen (1999), 'On Appropriation and Singularisation: Two Consumption Processes,' *Advances in Consumer Research*, vol. 26.

Magazines

Modern Bride 1992

Internet sites

www.findgift.com/Categories/Keepsake/Memory-Boxes (2006 – 01 – 16)

www.Familyjewelsarchivals.com (2005 – 08 – 15)

www.familyjewelsarchival.com/themeweddingdresskit.htm

www.indianchild.com/wedding

www.aimeej.com

www.personalizationmall.com

www.heelerandreid.com

www.rememberwhen.se/
www.lexmark.com/uncomplicate
www.Bridalpeople.com/memory

Biography

Helene Brembeck is an associate professor in Ethnology and research leader at the Center for Consumer Science (CFK). Her research interests are parenthood and childhood in consumer culture, also including food and eating, and she has published several books and anthologies in this field, e.g. 'Inte bara mamma' (Not just a mother) 1998, 'Det konsumerande barnet' (The Consuming Child) 2001 and 'Postmodern barndom' (Postmodern Childhood) 1996 together with Barbro Johansson. Together with Karin M. Ekström she is the editor of 'Elusive Consumption' (Berg 2004) and 'European Advances in Consumer Research, Vol. 7'. She has published articles in international journals, e.g. Ethnologia Scandinavica, Ethnologia Europeae and Food, Culture and Society, and in international anthologies, e.g. Gutman & de Coninck-Smith (eds.) 'Designing Modern Childhoods' (Rutgers University Press, in press).

Maria Brodin is a Ph.D. student in Business Administration at the Center for Consumer Science (CFK), Göteborg University. She is working on a dissertation on how contemporary dwellings are ordered through consumption and how 'homes' are produced and conceptualized in this process. Her research is concerned with the relationship between consumption, place and practice.

Karin M. Ekström is an associate professor in Business Administration, director and research leader at the Center for Consumer Science (CFK) School of Business, Economics & Law at Göteborg University. Her research concerns collecting, families and consumer socialization. Together with Helene Brembeck, she is the editor of 'Elusive Consumption' (Berg 2004) and 'European Advances in Consumer Research, vol. 7'. She is on the editorial review board for the Academy of Marketing Science Review, Consumption, Markets and Culture, Journal of Consumer Behaviour and Young Consumers. She is a member of the Royal Society of Arts and Sciences in Göteborg.

Lena Hansson is a Ph.D. in Business Administration at the Center for Consumer Science (CFK). She defended her thesis 'Universal design – a marketable or utopian concept?' in June, 2006. She is currently working on the inter-disciplinary project 'Design and Gender' and a post-doc-project focusing on the meaning of design for consumers 55+ and a social perspective on sustainability.

Barbro Johansson is an associate professor in Ethnology and researcher at the Center for Consumer Science (CFK). Her research interests are different aspects of modern childhood, such as media, consumption and children's rights. Some of her publications in the field are "'Kom och ät! Jag ska bara dö först": Datorn i barns vardag' (Time to eat! Okay, I'll just die first: The computer in children's everyday life) 2000, Barn i konsumtionssamhället (Children in consumer society) 2005. Together with Helene Brembeck she has been the editor of 'Postmodern barndom' (Postmodern childhood) 1996 and with Helene Brembeck and Jan Kampmann editor of the anthology 'Beyond the competent child' 2004. Currently she is working on a research project concerning children's food habits and another about child perspective in city planning.

Pernilla Jonsson holds a Ph.D. in Business Administration; specializing in consumer research. She defended her thesis 'Capturing the elusive simplifier' in June, 2006. She is currently the Director of the Consumer, Marketing & Innovation Department at the consultancy firm Kairos Future, and has also previous experience from the automobile industry as a management consultant and as a former employee of Saab Automobile AB.

Eva Knuts is a Ph.D. in Ethnology at the Center for Consumer Science (CFK), Göteborg University. She defended her thesis 'Something old, something new... – The creation of wedding performances' in October 2006. Her research interests are material culture, the body and gender and she has published articles on these issues in Swedish scientific journals, like Kulturella Perspektiv.

Magnus Mörck is an associate professor in Ethnology and research leader at the Center for Consumer Science (CFK). He is doing research in visual and material aspects of consumption including fashion and graphic design. Together with Magdalena Petersson he has edited a double issue of Kulturella Perspektiv 2005 (Cultural Perspectives), Scandinavia's leading periodical in Cultural Studies, on a wide range of studies on clothes and fashion. Together with Karin M. Ekström he edited the first full-length academic monograph on e-cinema, 'Skärpa på e-bion' (Focus on E-Cinema, Center for Consumer Science 2004).

Another book, 'Spel på ytan' (Surface Play) is a study on the lifestyles of cultural producers.

Alison J. Clarke is a Chair of Design History and Theory at the University of Applied Arts, Vienna. She has published widely on issues of gender, material culture, design and domesticity and is co-founder and co-editor of Home Cultures: The Journal of Architecture, Design and Domestic Space. She has just completed an extensive ethnographic research project of design and the domestic at AHCR centre for the Study of the Domestic Interior, Royal College of Art, London.

Kultur: Forschung und Wissenschaft

Riyan J. G. van den Born; Wouter T. de Groot; Rob H. J. Lenders (Eds.)
Visions of Nature
A scientific exploration of people's implicit philosophies regarding nature in Germany, the Netherlands and the United Kingdom
'Visions of nature' are the ideas that people hold of what nature is and how we should relate to it. These visions – besides being a dynamic cultural phenomenon worthy of scientific study for its own sake – are important for the design of democratically grounded landscape and nature policies. Drawing from a wide range of disciplines from the social sciences, the humanities and ecology, this volume reports on the growing scientific insights in visions of nature in Europe. Aspects covered are the long term dynamics of relationships between people and nature connected to land-use and urbanisation, landscape preferences related to views on nature, the structure and distribution of images such as stewardship of nature, partnership with nature and 'deep ecology' views, visions of nature as elicited in discussions with groups of adults and children, the role of emotional affinity to nature and of sudden disastrous events such as a river flood, the cultural construction of visions of nature through mass media and the ways in which ecologists translate their scientific visions of nature into criteria and images for policy making.
Bd. 4, 2006, 264 S., 29,90 €, br.,
ISBN 3-8258-9008-2

Transnational and Transatlantic American Studies

edited by
Mita Banerjee (Siegen),
Kornelia Freitag (Bochum),
Walter Grünzweig (Dortmund),
Randi Gunzenhäuser (Dortmund),
Rüdiger Kunow (Potsdam),
Wilfried Raussert (Bielefeld),
Michael Wala (Bochum)

Walter Grünzweig
The United States in Global Contexts
American Studies after 9/11 and Iraq
The momentous events since September 11, 2001, both challenged the field of American Studies and opened up new opportunities for research, teaching, and activism. This book presents more than 160 short contributions by Americanists and Non-Americanists from around the world in an essayistic brainstorm that brings together many questions asked about "America" and American Studies in the age of globalization. Die einschneidenden Veränderungen seit dem 11. September 2001 stellen für die Amerikanistik eine große Herausforderung dar, eröffnen aber auch neue Wege zu Forschung, Lehre und politischem Engagement. Die mehr als 160 Kurzbeiträge von Amerikanist/innen und Nicht-Amerikanist/innen aus vielen Teilen der Welt sind ein essayistischer brainstorm, der wichtige Fragen zu „Amerika" und zur Amerikanistik im Zeitalter der Globalisierung zusammenführt.
Bd. 1, 2004, 184 S., 19,90 €, br.,
ISBN 3-8258-8262-4

Aija Poikāne-Daumke
African Diasporas
Afro-German Literature in the Context of the African American Experience
This book investigates the development of Afro-German literature in the context of the African American experience and shows the decisive role of literature for the emergence of the Afro-German Movement. Various Afro-German literary and cultural initiatives, which began in the 1980s, arose as a response to

LIT Verlag Berlin – Hamburg – London – Münster – Wien – Zürich
Fresnostr. 2 48159 Münster
Tel.: 0251 – 62 032 22 – Fax: 0251 – 23 19 72
e-Mail: vertrieb@lit-verlag.de – http://www.lit-verlag.de

the experience of being marginalized – to the point of invisibility – within a dominant Eurocentric culture that could not bring the notions of „Black“ and „German“ together in a meaningful way. The book is a significant contribution to the understanding of German literature as multi-ethnic and of the the transatlantic networks operating in the African Diasporas.
Bd. 2, 2006, 144 S., 24,90 €, br.,
ISBN 3-8258-9612-9

Comparative Anthropological Studies in Society, Cosmology and Politics

ed. by
Prof. Dr. Josephus D. M. Platenkamp (University of Münster/Germany) and Prof. Dr. Bruce Kapferer (University of Bergen/Norway)

Guido Sprenger
Die Männer, die den Geldbaum fällten
Konzepte von Austausch und Gesellschaft bei den Rmeet von Takheung, Laos
Die seit 50 Jahren erste Monographie zu den Rmeet (Lamet), einer Hochlandgesellschaft in Laos, kreist um die Frage: Welche Beziehungen werden für notwendig erachtet, um die Gesellschaft zu reproduzieren? Dabei werden Rituale und der sozio-kosmische Gabentausch, der Personen, Häuser und Dörfer konstituiert, ebenso angesprochen wie Handel, Nationalstaat und interethnische Beziehungen. Durch die Verbindung klassischer ethnographischer Themen mit einer geschichts- und globalisierungsbewussten Perspektive entsteht das dynamische Bild eines lokalen Wertesystems.
Ausgezeichnet mit dem Förderpreis des Frobenius-Instituts 2004
Bd. 1, 2006, 344 S., 29,90 €, br.,
ISBN 3-8258-8043-5

John Christian Knudsen
Capricious Worlds
Vietnamese Life Journeys. With a Foreword by E. Valentine Daniel
"Capricious Worlds" covers a period of 20 years of exile. Through the life journeys of Vietnamese refugees, the book presents a world rich in experience and wisdom, where the will to survive is complemented by the skills to do so. Individuals must learn to conquer systems that transform human beings into numbers, and men, women and children into de-personalized figures. The transformations render an unsettling peace that refugees struggle against, inspired by a search for recognition, a search not only for what is lost, but also for what might yet be. The book is about refugees en route to, and in, Norway. It also speaks to the challenges of being exiled in general: a reality for 40 million refugees and internally displaced persons worldwide.
Bd. 2, 2005, 224 S., 24,90 €, br.,
ISBN 3-8258-8108-3

Paul van der Grijp
Passion and Profit
Towards an Anthropology of Collecting
Collecting is a matter of authenticity, of creating new identities, both of the objects collected and, by extension, of the collector. Passion and Profit provides a range of ethnographic examples, both historical and contemporary, and also includes a selective analysis and personal evaluation of the increasingly rich and varied literature on collecting. The collectibles discussed in Passion and Profit are not only elitist cultural objects such as works of art (ancient, modern or tribal), antiques and books, but also non-elitist objects such as stamps, postcards, plants, and other mass-produced items. The central research question is: What is the cultural phenomenon of collecting all about? Or, more specifically: What moves collectors? In addressing this question, this book aims to be a substantial contribution to the collecting literature from an anthropological point of view.
Bd. 3, 2006, 336 S., 29,90 €, br.,
ISBN 3-8258-9258-1